Then God Said

THEN GOD SAID

Contemplating the First Revelation in Creation

~

SUSAN MUTO

WIPF & STOCK · Eugene, Oregon

THEN GOD SAID
Contemplating the First Revelation in Creation

Wipf and Stock
An Imprint of Wipf and Stock Publishers
199 W. 8th Ave., Suite 3
Eugene, OR 97401

www.wipfandstock.com

ISBN 13: 978-1-62564-901-0

Manufactured in the U.S.A.   07/03/2014

The God who made the world and everything in it, he who is Lord of Heaven and Earth, does not live in shrines made by human hands, nor is he served by human hands, as though he needed anything, since he himself gives to all mortals life and breath and all things ... indeed he is not far from each one of us. For "in him we live and move and have our being ..." (Acts 17:24–28).

Contents

Part Three: Things Invested with Transcendent Meaning

Part Four: Places in Nature Pointing to God

Prologue

Inspiring the title of this book is the account of the six days of creation recorded at the beginning of the Book of Genesis. In these verses we contemplate the first revelation of God in Creation. We humans only came into being after a veritable avalanche of animate and inanimate creatures from first light and first night, to water and sky, land and every fruit-bearing plant and seed, to swarms of birds and animals populating the earth, to cattle and creeping things. And God saw that all of it was good. It was to be our duty as males and females created in his likeness to be the caretakers of this lush garden, to work and rest with God. Alas, prideful disobedience multiplied "thorns and thistles" (Gen 3:18); death entered the Garden of Eden, and with it shame and sin. But, to this day, when any of us feel distraught and distressed, we are likely to take a stroll along a shaded path or a walk by the sea, contemplating again the glory of the first revelation in creation and wondering, in a steel and cement world, why we do not do so more often.

Every epiphany of the mystery—human (you and I), cosmic (elemental), and trans-cosmic (divine)—connotes images and symbols illumined for us in and through this initial revelation. All three manifestations of the transcendent heighten our perception of the immense variety of forms and formations God uses to disclose the power of the Father, the presence of the Son, and the productivity of the Holy Spirit. My hope is that this book will serve as a wake-up call, alerting readers in all walks of life, from poets to entrepreneurs, to the majesty of this planet and to the merciful dispensation of the Divine under which we live from day to day.

Throughout history Christian believers and sincere seekers have turned to holy books, notably the Bible, to find validation for the link between what their senses behold and the hand that crafted the stars and calls them all by name (Ps 148:3). The masters tell us that the more we enjoy these epiphanic splendors, the more we come to know the Divine Giver who lavished them upon us. Thanks to the beauty we behold on earth and the sheer majesty of the universe beamed to us from the marvels of telescopic ingenuity, we find footprints of the love that moves the sun, the moon, and all the stars, as the poet Dante said of paradise. For mere mortals, what we see goes beyond speech and thought, and we are left stammering in "ah!" Still attempted articulations never cease.

For example, Hildegaard of Bingen (1098–1179) insists in her prose and poetry that all creatures mirror God in some manner. Brother Lawrence of the Resurrection (1611–1691), from whom we derive so many teachings on the practice of the presence of God, says that what launched his spiritual journey was a meditation on the wonder of a tree in winter. John Calvin (1509–1564), the great Protestant reformer from Switzerland, reminds us that there is no spot in the universe that does not overwhelm us with a spark of God's glory. As we read in Psalm 19:1, "The heavens are telling the glory of God; and the firmament proclaims his handiwork." Who could miss the great celebration of creation penned by Sirach (24:13–14) to tell us what our Creator is like? We need not look far to find the "I am" power of the self-communicating mystery: "I grew tall like a cedar in Lebanon, and like a cypress on the heights of Hermon. I grew tall like a palm tree in Engedi, and like rosebushes in Jericho; like a fair olive tree in the field, and like a plain tree growing beside water."

Returning to medieval times, Hugh of St. Victor (+1142) called creation the looking glass of God on which we ought to meditate day and night. Not only did Francis of Assisi (1182–1226) heed this advice; he took it a step further and in his Canticle of the Sun embraced all facets of creation as his brothers and sisters. His successor, Bonaventure (1221–1274), in his treatise on the journey of the mind to God (1259), writes that anyone not enlightened by the splendor of created things must be blind. He says, " . . . open your eyes, alert the ears of your spirit, open your lips and apply your heart so that in all creatures you may see, hear, praise, love and worship, glorify and honor your God . . . " In the same vein, the Book of Wisdom (1:14) says: "For he created all things so that they might exist; the generative forces of the world are wholesome, and there is not a destructive poison in them . . . "

Creation not only reminds us of God's glory; it offers us a sacramental understanding of earth, air, fire, and water, of all the elements in nature and culture. These gifts that unroll without price at our feet delight the eye. They are not God, but they are valued by us as God's creation deserving of our love and respect. When the English poet, Alfred Lord Tennyson (1850–1892) saw a "flower in a crannied wall," he almost swooned in wonder. Reading in awe the book of nature heightened his sensitivity to the truth that . . . "every perfect gift is from above, coming down from the Father of lights, with whom there is no variation or shadow due to change" (Jas 1:17).

Contact with nature—on a scale as small as a dandelion peeking through a crack in the sidewalk or as gigantic as the Grand Canyon seen for the first time—restores our faded, jaded outlook on life; imparts peace to an agitated mind; and reconfirms the awesome splendor of beauty and order, destined, as the Bible says, to glorify God, the author of all that delights our eyes and ears, our senses of smell, taste and touch. The next time we behold the first blooms of spring, inhale the air heavy with the scent of lilacs, or bite into a perfectly ripe crunchy apple, we, too, can celebrate the first revelation of God in creation. For the contemporary poet, Gerard Manley Hopkins (1844–1889), the world is charged with the grandeur of God. A glance in any direction will prove his point. Reflected in everything from a butterfly's wing to the soaring Alps are traces of Infinite Beauty. Is there any doubt that Mother Earth is the house of God and the gateway to heaven?

I am indebted throughout this book both for information and inspiration to insights and illustrations found in the *Dictionary of Biblical Imagery*, General Editors: Leland Ryken, James C. Wilhoit, and Tremper Longman III (Downers Grove, Illinois: Intervarsity Press, 1998). My preferred source of biblical quotes is the New Revised Standard Version (NRSV). Grateful appreciation also goes to the faculty and staff of the Epiphany Association and its Board of Directors for their generous editorial and financial support, all of which helped to bring this labor of love to completion.

As we begin reading this tribute to creation and the respectful stewardship that is so much a part of today's concern for ecological spirituality, let us pause for a moment and pray with the psalmist:

> Praise the Lord from the earth,
>   you sea monsters and all deeps,
> fire and hail, snow and frost,
>   stormy wind fulfilling his command!
> Mountains and all hills,
>   fruit trees and all cedars!
> Wild animals and all cattle,
>   creeping things and flying birds!
>
> Kings of the earth and all peoples,
>   princes and all rulers of the earth!
> Young men and women alike,
>   old and young together!
>
> Let them praise the name of the Lord,
>   for his name alone is exalted;
>   his glory is above earth and heaven.
> He has raised up a horn for his people,
>   praise for all his faithful,
>   for the people of Israel who are close to him.
> Praise the Lord! (Ps 148:7–14)

PART ONE

Animals Beloved by God
That Bow Before God's Face

1.

Birds

Ps 50:10–11. For every wild animal of the forest is mine, the cattle on a thousand hills. I know all the birds of the air, and all that moves in the field is mine.

Matt 6:26. Look at the birds of the air; they neither sow nor reap nor gather into barns, and yet your heavenly Father feeds them.

At one moment or another all of us have probably dreamt of what it would be like to soar free as a bird in the blue sky, flitting from branch to branch, not as random creatures in an indifferent cosmos but as spirits known intimately by our Creator, who feeds us season by season and guides our migratory flights.

Picture any bird—from a red-breasted robin to an American eagle—and the first word that comes to mind is freedom. The second a predator approaches, wings arch, spread, flap and this beautifully formed creature flies away.

Birds display a remarkable diversity within the unity of flight. They flit like sandpipers with the ebb and flow of the sea. They coo like doves announcing the dawn of a new day and squawk like crows disturbing our peace. They announce with excited chirps the shift from winter to spring and migrate over distances that defy the imagination.

Homing pigeons carry messages from senders to recipients, who may not have access to any other means of communication. Birds are plain as sparrows and as rainbow-hued as rare rain forest parrots. Some are seen as bearers of good omens like white pigeons; others as harbingers of death and destruction like buzzards and vultures.

As any bird watcher may be inclined to conclude, they are living books the Creator may use to teach us lessons we are not likely to forget. Birds of prey can symbolize impending, indeed ominous, signs of divine judgment (Hos 8:1). None of us want to be doomed creatures who fall to their death in the "snare of the fowler" (Ps 91:4). How much better it is to "fly away and be at rest" (Ps 55:6), to live the worry-free existence of winged wonders who neither sow nor reap (Luke 12:24). Birds trust in the daily bread supplied by Providence (Ps 147:9) and so ought we. Isn't it ironic that they build nests wherever they are while so many of us humans are homeless (Luke 9:58)? Under their wings we find a symbol of divine protection (Ps 63:7) from malevolent spirits and a place where we can pause a while and restore our strength.

Birds teach us lessons about fidelity. Some, like ospreys, mate for life. From others, we learn the meaning of nurturing as when a mother bird, at risk to herself, feeds and protects her young. No matter how far away we roam, birds teach us that homecoming is always a reachable goal. In Aesop's fable, *The Stork and the Farmer*, the stork argues that it should be set free to go home and take care of its parents in their old age, and the farmer agrees. By contrast, the seeming indifference of ostriches to their offspring is an unacceptable model for good parent-child relationships (Lam 4:3).

Birds convey many messages, ranging from picking at a carcass and chasing away its competitors to reminding us what it means to protect our young and spread seeds in fertile soil. Their examples of loyalty evoke our admiration, their beauty our awe, and so we pray: *"Lord, let me live as fully and freely as possible in fidelity to your call until that day when my soul, on wings of dawn, flies through the cage of time to its homecoming in eternity."*

2.

Colts

Zech 9:9. Rejoice greatly, O daughter Zion! Shout aloud, O daughter Jerusalem! Lo, your king comes to you, triumphant and victorious is he, humble and riding on a donkey, on a colt, the foal of a donkey.

John 12:14–5. Jesus found a young donkey and sat on it; as it is written: 'Do not be afraid, daughter of Zion. Look, your king is coming, sitting on a donkey's colt!'

"You jackass!" has always been a pejorative expletive and yet the lowly colt has played a significant role in salvation history and in the progress of humanity. This low-maintenance beast of burden provided a means of transportation for poor people, tackled treacherous terrains, and earned a reputation for being worth its weight in gold. Everyone knows that mules and donkeys and colts can be stubborn creatures, at times adamantly refusing to move without the application of the whip, but their reliability and resilience are unquestionable.

Lowly as it was the donkey was destined to become in scriptural lore a mount of nobility. It was the animal of choice that would transport Mary, heavy with child, to Bethlehem. In nativity productions, Joseph gently guides the mule carrying the mother of our Lord and Savior. Its breath and body warm the stable where she gave birth. At other times, donkeys bore a great deal of abuse, being whipped senseless and accused of being dumb, but nothing could be farther from the truth. This sure-footed creature not only mastered dizzying trails like those that carry tourists deep into the Grand Canyon but also became a sign of an impending ascension to power as when David mounted Solomon on his own mule (I Kgs 1:33).

Similarly, Jesus orchestrated his triumphal entry into Jerusalem not on a majestic war horse but on a lowly mule, regarded in that scene as a symbol of kingship and peace (Matt 21:2). Neither swaying palm branches nor loud hosannas could break this beast's steady pace through the cobblestone streets of Jerusalem. Imagine, if this colt could talk, what a story it would tell! Just as Jesus raised up the donkey's dignity at the time of his birth and shortly before his death, so he wants to lift up the likes of us. It is not the mule's stubbornness we are to emulate but the patience with which it accepts and carries the weight placed on it. Revealed in this ordinary beast is a knack for efficiency that might arouse our envy. That the Lord himself rode on it conveys the truth that he often chooses the nothings of this world to do his will.

Once upon a time there was an old monk who had a scripture quote for whatever happened in the monastery—a habit the younger monks wanted him to break. The abbot agreed with them and chastised the erstwhile biblical expert to kneel in perfect silence in the middle of the refectory during meals. He accepted his punishment with docility, but one day the beast of burden became untethered and ran toward the dining area braying at the top of its lungs. The monks jumped up in an attempt to restrain it and silence this outrageous disruption of their table.

When the commotion stopped and the monks returned to the dining room, they found the old monk doubled over with laughter. The abbot beckoned him to approach and said in a rather haughty tone, "Well, my brother, if you can find a scriptural quote to cover what just happened your penance will be remitted by me." The accused raised his eyes to heaven, folded his hands, and said in a somber tone, "He came unto his own and his own received him not." With the truth having been told, he returned to his place, ate in silence, and tried not to notice the understandably mortified monks on either side of him. Was it not Saint Francis of Assisi who described his own body as "Brother Ass." Yet it was this very body that Jesus honored by imprinting upon it his own wounds, and so we pray: *"Lord, in this often dense and dreary life, let me follow that donkey that bore you amidst hosannas to the Last Supper, thus fulfilling the prophecy that 'your king is coming to you, humble, and mounted on a donkey, and on a colt, the foal of a donkey' (Matt 21:5). On this journey from death to life, create a new heart in me that I may not return stubbornly to all that used to be."*

3.

Goats

Ps 50:12–14. If I were hungry, I would not tell you, for the world and all that is in it is mine. Do I eat the flesh of bulls, or drink the blood of goats? Offer to God a sacrifice of thanksgiving, and pay your vows to the Most High.

Heb 10:4–6. For it is impossible for the blood of bulls and goats to take away sins. Consequently, when Christ came into the world, he said, 'Sacrifices and offerings you have not desired, but a body you have prepared for me; in burnt-offerings and sin-offerings you have taken no pleasure.

Both in scripture and by virtue of our own observations, goats often convey a double meaning. On the one hand, they seem to embody our fallen condition as when the Son of Man separates the righteous sheep from the cursed goats (Matt 25: 31–46). On the other hand, they are depicted throughout the Bible as the animals of choice offered to God as sacrifices or burnt offerings, symbolizing both atonement and adoration.

Goats were a sin-offering from the people to the Lord (Lev 16:29–34). Once slaughtered, their blood was transported to a holy place while their carcass was hauled outside the camp and burned.

In the New Testament, there is a comparison recorded in the book of Hebrews to symbolize the costly death of Jesus Christ, who "suffered outside the city gate in atonement for our sins" (Heb 13:12). Once this sacrifice was finished, Jesus ascended in mystical adoration and sat at the right hand of the Father (Heb 10:12).

In the Old Testament, the goat also became the "scapegoat" (Lev 16:8). All the sins of Israel were piled on the goat's head, and it was sent away into the desert. This symbol, too, was applied to Christ, who took our sins upon himself and removed them from us. No sacrifice could have been greater than this act of selfless love on the crucible of the cross.

Another facet of this creature is its witness of wild abandonment as when mountain goats tackle climbs over rocky terrain as if it were a smooth highway. They leap from slope to slope almost without touching the ground. The prophet Daniel saw a great goat attacking a huge ram, signifying a rival empire and trampling on him (Dan 8:5–8). Goats are not only submissive but also agile symbols of powerful leadership. When the true Prince of Peace comes among us he tells us that he is not pleased with the blood of bulls and goats because what he seeks is not sacrifice but mercy.

Once again, scripture presents goats as a mixed breed—at once carriers of sacrifice for sin and symbols of forgiveness. We can be foolish goats who refuse to follow God's design for our lives and rush headlong toward ultimate destruction or docile creatures who give God free reign over our destiny. After all, goats' hair was a source of cloth as valuable to nomads as cashmere to princes.

Recall that the enraptured lover in Solomon's Song compares the hair of his beloved to that of "a flock of goats, moving down the slopes of Gilead" (Song 4:1; 6:5). Then, too, the flesh of roasted goats and their nourishing milk feeds hungry people the world over. Goats are among the best provisions nature supplies.

My maternal grandmother, who grew up in the hills of Calabria, Italy, reminded us that one goat was enough to prevent a whole family from having to face starvation. When a mother could not nurse her baby, goat's milk was the drink of choice to help the child grow. In a country like Mexico, goat's meat roasted with spices is a delicacy. Guests offered this treat relish its flavor, a truth I can personally verify thanks to my travels south of the border, and so we pray: *"Lord, despite the temptations to fall into infidelity, grant me the grace to surrender my will to the pervasive mystery of your will for me. Let me abide by its slow unfolding, especially when life demands a positive response to the rigors inherent in any faith journey."*

4.

Horses

Exod 15:1–2. Then Moses and the Israelites sang this song to the Lord:
'I will sing to the Lord, for he has triumphed gloriously;
horse and rider he has thrown into the sea.
The Lord is my strength and my might,
and he has become my salvation;
this is my God, and I will praise him,
my father's God, and I will exalt him.'

Rev 19 11–13. Then I saw heaven opened, and there was a white horse! Its rider is called Faithful and True, and in righteousness he judges and makes war. His eyes are like a flame of fire, and on his head are many diadems; and he has a name inscribed that no one knows but himself. He is clothed in a robe dipped in blood, and his name is called the Word of God.

From battlefield formations to circus rings, from military parades to world famous races, horses signify power and beauty, speed and agility, affection, and loyalty. Expert "horse whisperers" tame them when they are wild and ready them for service in farms, fields, and stables across the world. When foes heard the thunder of hoofs and the neighing of horses, they knew they were about to begin a fight to the finish. As we read in 1 Kgs 20:23, mounted cavalry and chariots "gave overwhelming superiority in battle, especially on the plains."

Thanks to God's care for the chosen people, Pharaoh and all his horses and chariots were no more powerful than toy soldiers. God opened the Red Sea to save Israel and then closed it over their persecutors (Exod 15:4). David and other Old Testament warriors kept enough horses to feel safe and secure from the most vicious of foes. Solomon's mounts numbered four hundred (2 Chr 9:25) and grew to as many as forty thousand (1 Kgs 4:26). Yet even these fierce four-legged creatures, companions of agile fighters, capable of running with the speed of the wind, had to bow to a Higher Power. Once tamed, a wild horse knows and obeys its master.

In ancient times, horses were often incorporated into statues of idols (Jer 5:8). They were seen as potent symbols of raw desire (like a *stud* or a *stallion*). This animal epitomized both military might and reproductive prowess. Experts trained them to win races, to jump over fences, and to put the fear of God in less expert riders. Horses are the favored animals of every civilization, but fighting the enemy is not their only purpose. They are friendly enough to nuzzle one's hand for a treat like a sugar cube or an apple. They may appear to be broken down hags but, as the famous story of Sea Biscuit reveals, they have remarkable staying-power, offering hope for rebirth to every "come-back kid."

In a great reversal of the bellicosity associated with horses in the Old Testament, we read that when the Lord establishes his reign of peace, warhorses will disappear from the streets of Jerusalem (Zech 9:10). While the Lord himself is depicted, for example in Hab 3:8, as a Divine Warrior, his aim is to protect his people and even in imaginary ways cause an enemy to run away in panic (2 Kgs 7:6).

This creature also appears in eschatological visions as when the Apostle John in the Book of Revelation (6:1–8) saw four horsemen riding different colored horses—white for the outbreak of a war of conquest; red for bloodshed; black for famine; pale for death. Then, in a later vision, the Son of Man and the heavenly troops he leads appear on white horses, riding forth to conquer God's foes. Those fools who persist in sin are like stubborn horses in need of being tamed for God's grace to flow through them (Ps 32:9), and so we pray: *"Lord, carry me beyond my idols. Walk with me in the softening light of simplicity of heart, of single-mindedness from which flows forth your presence like fresh water from a spring. Eternal Other, forgotten Source, mysterious core, tend in me the tender flower of holy presence that gently blooms in the mild and even climate of equanimity!"*

5.

Lambs

Isa 53:7. He was oppressed, and he was afflicted,
yet he did not open his mouth;
like a lamb that is led to the slaughter,
and like a sheep that before its shearers is silent,
so he did not open his mouth.

Rev 5:11–12. Then I looked, and I heard the voice of
many angels surrounding the throne and the living creatures and the elders; they numbered myriads of myriads
and thousands of thousands, singing with full voice,
'Worthy is the Lamb that was slaughtered
to receive power and wealth and wisdom and might
and honor and glory and blessing!'

Remember the nursery rhyme, "Mary had a little lamb, its fleece was white as snow, and everywhere that Mary went, the lamb was sure to go." These beloved creatures receive nearly two hundred biblical references, depicting such character dispositions as gentleness, innocence, and dependence on God. Docile disciples of the Lord emulate the Lamb of God, who will take them in his arms because they are helpless without him (Isa 40:11). Lambs obey their keepers; they have no inclination to resist their call when they so much as whistle. One of the most startling predictions in the writings of the prophet Isaiah (65:25) is that lambs will lie with wolves when God's kingdom comes to fruition.

Lambs are also sacrificial symbols, willingly led to the slaughter (Jer 15:40). Such will be the destiny of the Suffering Servant, whose only wish is to say *yes* to the Father's will. Powerless as lambs are, only *the* Lamb can release us from the bondage of sin. This image of our own and others' vulnerability evokes compassion. There is no point in denying our weakness. It prompts us to trust in the empowering strength that will be given to us by the Lord, who sends us into the fields as lambs, innocent and guileless. Though we are surrounded by the wolves of lust, greed, anger, gluttony and envy, we shall not—by the Lord's promise—be devoured (Luke 10:3). This motif of sacrifice reaches its culmination in Christ, the Paschal Lamb (I Cor 5:7) "without defect or blemish" (I Pet 1:19) whose blood will wash us clean of sin and allow us, garbed in white robes, to forever sing the praises of God.

Lambs signify the saving power of the Lord as well as the longing every soul feels when he or she pleads to be found. "Amazing grace, how sweet the sound that saved a wretch like me, I once was lost, but now am found, once blind and now I see." When lambs wander off, the shepherd's first thought is to rescue them; his main aim is to shield them from danger. Jesus says of the Good Shepherd, who has a hundred sheep, that he will leave the ninety-nine behind in the wilderness and go after the one who is lost, not ceasing his search until he finds this stray (Luke 15:4).

Artists often depict Jesus with a lamb wrapped around his neck or cradled in his arms. Maybe as a child he played with these gentle, trusting creatures. Did he have a chance to watch them leap with abandonment across the fields around Nazareth and the Sea of Galilee? Perhaps their "baa-baa" moans aroused his concern. They sounded as frightened as youngsters would when darkness falls and they find themselves alone.

Lambs need protection in this land of ravenous wolves and so do we. There is no use pretending we can navigate the woods and marshlands where danger lurks without a Good Shepherd to guide us. There is no shame in being so dependent, for where Jesus goes we are sure to follow, and so we pray: *"Lord, quiet my restless ruminations and hold me like a lamb in your arms. Whisper to my wayward heart the humble truth that life is a mystery to be lived, not a problem to be solved. Teach me to be at home with the ambiguity that when I am as weak as a baby lamb I am strong in you. With frolicking wonder, let me abandon myself to what is beyond the complexity that assails my agitated mind. Unbind me from the fear that forestalls faith and lead me to the fertile pasture of your presence."*

6.

Lions

Dan 6:19–22. Then, at break of day, the king got up and hurried to the den of lions. When he came near the den where Daniel was, he cried out anxiously to Daniel, 'O Daniel, servant of the living God, has your God whom you faithfully serve been able to deliver you from the lions?' Daniel then said to the king, 'O king, live forever! My God sent his angel and shut the lions' mouths so that they would not hurt me, because I was found blameless before him; and also before you, O king, I have done no wrong.'

2 Tim 4:17–18. But the Lord stood by me and gave me strength, so that through me the message might be fully proclaimed and all the Gentiles might hear it. So I was rescued from the lion's mouth. The Lord will rescue me from every evil attack and save me for his heavenly kingdom. To him be the glory for ever and ever. Amen.

On a trip I made to Tanzania to lecture on formative spirituality, an afternoon break provided me with a rare opportunity. My host asked me if I had ever seen lions in the wild. I answered "no," with an unmistakable spark of interest in my eyes, and without hesitation he arranged for a short safari to a nearby wildlife preserve. Good fortune smiled upon us, for there in the hot afternoon sun we spotted a pride of lions whose majesty matched the awe we felt. That age-old gaze of the jungle king reduced us to silence and reminded us of how vulnerable we really are.

The Israelites viewed lions as ruthless, unstoppable killers ravaging their flocks at will and evoking terror: "The lion has roared; who will not fear?" (Amos 3:8). One can hardly imagine the gory scene in the Roman Coliseum when the early Christian martyrs were fed to hungry lions. Reportedly, they met these beasts singing with joy since they were the instruments assuring their passage to eternal salvation. There was no physical escape from the mouth of the lion (Heb 11:33), but what these believers longed for was spiritual release.

Scripture portrays the devil as a roaring lion seeking whom he may devour (I Pet 5:8) and depicts, by contrast, God's lion-like strength and avenging power (Prov 28:1). The lion also serves as a symbol of royalty, frequently carved in stone to bestow shades of glory on members of a royal household like that of Judah (Gen 49:9 and Ezek 19:2.9). Whenever Israel triumphs over its foes, it is seen as fit as a lion devouring its prey (Num 23:24); when the opposite occurs and glory fades, the prophet depicts enslaved people as helpless as lions trapped in a snare (Ezek 19:8–9). The stark contrast of a lion's existence—killer and prey, hunter and hunted—represents a people in its prime and in its decline.

Lions embody the truth that no animal, not even the king of the jungle, can survive on its own. Animals as wild and proud as they are depend on the prey they stalk to provide the sustenance they need. All creatures, this carnivorous one included, remain under God's control. At the bidding of the Divine, lions may one day lie down with lambs (Isa 11:6). A key messianic prophecy reveals that in the end the conquest of evil will not occur by means of destructive bludgeoning but by constructive obedience (Rev 5:5–6).

Our lion king, Jesus Christ, is there to protect us when we are most in need. He greets us with a steady gaze of love. His wisdom outrivals that of any other God and so great is his strength that he will overcome death. Christ greets us not with a terrifying roar but with an inviting whisper, "Come to me." There is not one malicious bone in his crucified and glorified body. Our lion king weans us away from the myth of self-sufficiency and reminds us of our reliance on God's providential care (Ps 34:10). The devil in his wickedness may be eager to tear us apart (Ps 17:12), but he is no match for the loving redeemer whose only desire is to heal our wounds and carry us home, and so we pray: *"Lord, let the stream of your love flow into the parched tundra of my often failing life. Like the fierce lion you are, break through the last remnants of my resistance. Fill me to the brink with your redeeming grace and heal this otherwise doomed land that I am with your divine word."*

7.

Serpents

Num 21:7–9. The people came to Moses and said, 'We have sinned by speaking against the Lord and against you; pray to the Lord to take away the serpents from us.' So Moses prayed for the people. And the Lord said to Moses, 'Make a poisonous serpent, and set it on a pole; and everyone who is bitten shall look at it and live.' So Moses made a serpent of bronze, and put it upon a pole; and whenever a serpent bit someone, that person would look at the serpent of bronze and live.

Matt 10:16–19. See, I am sending you out like sheep into the midst of wolves; so be wise as serpents and innocent as doves. . .when they hand you over, do not worry about how you are to speak or what you are to say; for what you are to say will be given to you at that time; for it is not you who speak but the spirit of your Father speaking through you.

Most of us shy away from snakes, preferring to view them behind glass in a zoo rather than meet them in the wild. We tend to forget that ancient cultures like the Mayan numbered serpents among their most prestigious "gods" and replicated them in elaborate stone carvings on their palaces and temples. Perhaps our generally repulsive reaction goes back to the Book of Genesis where the serpent is the symbol of demonic seduction (Gen 3:1). Anyone who does the devil's bidding is from then on referred to as a snake (Matt 3:7). Their words are like venomous poison (Ps 140:3); they are never to be trusted since they threaten us with greater evils (Isa 59:5). Snake charmers seem to exert power over poisonous serpents but one wrong move may mean their death. Their bites were so bad that Moses needed a miraculous staff to rescue the chosen people crossing the desert from swarms of vipers (Exod 4:4 and Num 21:9).

Yet serpents are also paradoxical creatures, both subtle like the snake that tempted Eve to eat the apple and wise (Matt 10:16) enough to proliferate not only in rain forests but backyard gardens where nature uses some of them to control, for example, the rodent population. Some snakes secrete venom so toxic it can kill a person in a matter of minutes but the same spittle properly treated can exude healing powers.

It is this contrast between evil and good that gives serpents an indelible place in our imagination. For example, shedding skin that does not suit a snake anymore may symbolize that the end of one era of life marks the beginning of the next. By their sinuous slithering they may hypnotize their prey and bite without warning. (Gen 49:17), reminding us that there is no escape from the swift and sudden judgment of the Divine (Isa 49:29; Amos 5:19).

The only person powerful enough to subdue the serpent is the woman clothed with the sun (Rev 12:1), who will step on the head of this dealer of death. She, along with her Son, will restore the balance of nature, moving us from dread to reverence for our saving God. We recall the prophecy of Isaiah (11:8) that innocent children will play without fear "over the hole of the asp."

This intertwining of the natural and the supernatural invites us to view salvation history in its entirety. No sooner does evil appear to triumph than what is good wins the day. As followers of Christ, we live in anticipation of the era when his victory is assured

(Mark 16:18). God's revelation in creation through the serpent lets us feel the tension between danger and opportunity, despair and hope. The situation in which we find ourselves seldom has a purely black or white meaning. We live in that gray area of ambiguity where the dictum that we are to be at one and the same time wise as serpents and gentle as doves makes perfect sense, and so we pray: *"Lord, in the push and pull of daily life, let me move with grace from darkness to dawn, from the terror of poisonous hate to the beauty of pure love, from the sting of evil to the victorious splendor of the good. Let me see my fragile frame through your eyes as a shrine of saving surrender for whom momentary affliction prepares me 'for an eternal weight of glory beyond all measure . . .'"* (2 Cor 4:17).

PART TWO

Fruits, Vegetables, Flowers, and Minerals Manifesting the Most High

1.

Clay

Jer 18:5–6. Then the word of the Lord came to me: Can I not do with you, O house of Israel, just as this potter has done? says the Lord. Just like the clay in the potter's hand, so are you in my hand, O house of Israel.

2 Cor 4:7–9. But we have this treasure in clay jars, so that it may be made clear that this extraordinary power belongs to God and does not come from us. We are afflicted in every way, but not crushed; perplexed, but not driven to despair; persecuted, but not forsaken; struck down, but not destroyed; always carrying in the body the death of Jesus, so that the life of Jesus may also be made visible in our bodies.

Consider the pliability of clay. Give a lump of it to a child or an artist and odd as well as elegant shapes appear. In the hands of a potter, this humble element can be transformed into an object of beauty, from a wall hanging to a complete set of dinnerware. Clay is a substance that accepts the impression etched or carved into it. In the scriptures it becomes an excellent metaphor for all of us as the work of God's hand (Isa 64:8; Jer 18:6). Into our clay the

Creator molds the unique form he wants us to manifest. Clay is so pliable it can be refined, reformed, and refashioned. Unlike marble that has to be hammered and chiseled before the polished product emerges, clay adapts to the creative shape the artist envisions.

If God is the master potter and we are the clay, then the form we take conforms to the purpose God has in mind for us. We become God-molded, docile people, obedient to God's perfect forming, reforming, and transforming plan for our lives. Perhaps that is why a man like Moses, powerful as he was, bears the accolade of being meek, which means to be God-molded.

In the same vein, we read in Psalm 37:11 that the meek shall inherit the land, a promise repeated by Jesus in the Sermon on the Mount (Matt 5:5). This character disposition, along with kindness, humility, and patience (Col 3:12), makes us better recipients of God's word. Clay does not resist the hand that shapes it and neither ought we to refuse to consent to our divine destiny.

Flexible and fresh as clay is, it can dry up and become brittle, comparable to that state of hard-heartedness that needs to be melted down in the crucible of meaningful suffering. The image God wants us to become is not prefabricated. In the clay that we humans are is a special element called free will. We can choose to remain instruments shaped by a love relationship with our Maker or stubborn souls who want to control their fate. The latter vision of obedience to our unique-communal call from God reminds us that from the same raw material an endless variety of goods can be made—from rustic vases to rare artifacts. Each of these objects conveys a solidity the user or the beholder can count upon. Other materials like glass are more breakable. Clay has staying-power complemented by a certain fragility, especially before it is fired.

Despite the care and craftsmanship of the sculptor, flaws may be found, but in certain schools of pottery the cracks and fault lines in the final product are what give it its unique beauty. Clay vessels can outlast the ages and store treasures as awesome as the Dead Sea Scrolls. At Cana in Galilee the six clay water jars were granted the honor of being the site of Jesus' first public miracle

(John 2:4–11). The wine poured from them was the best the wedding host had to offer.

In some sense, it is an honor for us to be made of clay and to have Jesus remind us, in addition to its adaptability, of its healing power. No sooner had he applied mud-like clay to the eyes of a blind man than he could see. (John 9:6–15), and so we pray: *"Lord, as my days speed hastily to their end, I know that life will collapse; my jar will be broken. Remind me with each chip of the aging process that you alone remain the everlasting one in whom I and others share. In spite of countless failings, you still hand me the chalice of your blood from which to drink, and the precious plate of your flesh from which to eat.*

2.

Figs

Hab 3:17–19. Though the fig tree does not blossom,
and no fruit is on the vines;
though the produce of the olive fails
and the fields yield no food;
though the flock is cut off from the fold
and there is no herd in the stalls,
yet I will rejoice in the Lord;
I will exult in the God of my salvation.
God, the Lord, is my strength;
he makes my feet like the feet of a deer,
and makes me tread upon the heights.

Matt 24:32–35. From the fig tree learn its lesson: as soon
as its branch becomes tender and puts forth its leaves,
you know that summer is near. So also, when you see all
these things, you know that he is near, at the very gates.
Truly I tell you, this generation will not pass away until
all these things have taken place. Heaven and earth will
pass away, but my words will not pass away.

When succulent figs flourish, they signify abundant life. The opposite outcome, symbolic death, looms when fig trees wither. In

the Genesis account of the Fall, innocence came to an end when Adam and Eve felt shame and attempted to cover their nakedness with fig leaves (Gen 3:7). So figs and fig trees like many biblical symbols convey a double meaning: plenty and poverty, protection and exposure, obedience and disobedience, fruitful yielding to the Most High and withering resistance.

No one can deny that figs are a wonderful food, as tasty fresh as dried. Used as appetizers or desserts, they are delicious compliments to any meal. The sunny, dry climate of Palestine was a perfect place to cultivate them for food as well as for shade, thus offering a ready symbol for the covenant relationship between us and God. "Seeing the early fruit on the fig tree" (Hos 9:10) manifests the promise of the fruitfulness that is the best by-product of this relationship. The withering of a fig tree is a danger sign of a spiritually unfruitful life (Luke 13:6–9). Disaster looms if this condition persists. Jesus uses the image of a barren fig tree that still has leaves to reveal that a religion that is all show and no substance lacks value; it may attract God's wrath because its proponents bear no tasty fruit in their lives (Mark 11:12–21).

A fruit bearing, leafy fig tree in a hot climate is as much a source of shade as of succulent nourishment. In the growing season, crows no sooner pick away at one fig than it produces another. A well fertilized, properly pruned tree symbolizes a settled life. Since a fig tree requires several years of labor to establish, to sit in its shade gives one the feeling that all is well despite the tension of want and plenty.

When the King of Assyria tempted Israel not to listen to the prophets and bow to him instead, he painted into this taunting picture what else but a fig tree, saying, "Make peace with me . . . then everyone of you will eat from his own vine and fig tree and drink water from his own cistern."(Isa 36:16). Prophets like Micah and Zechariah hold to the promise that this tree has an eternal as well as a temporal role to play. It will be part of the eschaton, of the new order God will establish in heaven and on earth, offering us evidence of the divine domesticity we are destined to enjoy: "In that day each of you will invite his neighbor to sit under his vine and fig tree." So declares the Lord Almighty (Zec 3:10; Mic 4:4).

Such an ancient tree symbolizes how even in the modern age we have the privilege of serving the coming of God's reign, and so we pray: *"Lord, inspired by this leafy tree, let me live with joyful vitality from winter to spring. May no adversity deter my course, may no defect slow my advance to that land of plenty that teems with the fruit of your tender care."*

3.

Gold

Job 28:12–15. But where shall wisdom be found?
And where is the place of understanding?
Mortals do not know the way to it,
and it is not found in the land of the living.
The deep says, "It is not in me,"
and the sea says, "It is not with me."
It cannot be bought for gold,
and silver cannot be weighed out as its price.

I Pet 6–9. In this you rejoice, even if now for a little while you have had to suffer various trials, so that the genuineness of your faith—being more precious than gold that, though perishable, is tested by fire—may be found to result in praise and glory and honor when Jesus Christ is revealed. Although you have not seen him, you love him; and even though you do not see him now, you believe in him and rejoice with an indescribable and glorious joy, for you are receiving the outcome of your faith, the salvation of your souls.

This metal is so precious and so bound to kingship that it was the first of the three gifts (gold, frankincense, and myrrh) the Magi offered to the Christ Child in Bethlehem. As lasting as it is beautiful to behold, gold adorned the temple and the tabernacle. Nothing but its splendor was good enough for God.

Yet this same treasure chipped from the bowels of the earth is the greedy soul's greatest temptation and the grossest source of idolatry. Remember that the Israelites built a golden calf while Moses received the tablets of stone into which were carved God's commandments (Exod 32:4).

On the razor's edge of the human condition, gold brings out both the best and worst in us. Distributed fairly, it sustains our economy and gives value to our currency. Amassed ruthlessly by robbers, murderers, and tyrants, it can devastate trust, destroy relationships, and lead whole populations to ruin.

The possession of gold may grant under noble circumstances wealth without viciousness as witnessed in Old Testament figures like Abraham (Gen 13:2; Esth 8:15) and Solomon (2 Chr 1:15). In the New Testament, Jesus reveals, what the Apostle Paul later confirms, than the love of money—not currency itself—is the root of all evil (1 Tim 6:10). Judas betrayed Jesus for thirty pieces of silver (Matt 26:15). The superior value of gold and why its possession is so problematic has to do with its permanence. Unlike silver, it does not tarnish. That is why pagan images were more often than not made of it. However shining its glory it, too, can fall as the destruction of Herod's temple proves. Still, good people are more worthwhile than gold whereas bad ones turn out to be as worthless as cracked glass.

The value biblical writers place on gold is proportionate to its representation not of human wealth but of the Almighty himself. In the Song of Songs, the Beloved's head, arms, and feet are covered with gold (Song 5:11, 14, 15). The psalmist says that God's laws are more precious than the finest displays of gold (Ps 19:10). Jesus issues a scathing question to the Pharisees who tried to trap him, saying "You blind fools! Which is great: the gold, or the temple that makes the gold sacred?" (Matt 23:16–17). Once again the misuse of gold can be the cause of serious immorality—from the making of idols to the oppression of the poor.

Gold, in accordance with the Gospel, needs to flow from our fingers, not to be grasped by them. Perhaps that is why Peter refers to faith as being of greater worth than gold, for while it may survive the refining process, it, too, perishes like any other finite entity. The purity of gold melted in a furnace is seen in scripture not as an end in itself, but as a metaphor for the way our hearts must be tested in the fire of God's love.

Though the streets of heaven may be paved in "pure gold" (Rev 21:18), it is useless to make this mineral a substitute for God. Mister Scrooge in Charles Dickens' *A Christmas Carol*, had to find out that gold becomes most valuable not when it is clung to in a miserly fashion but when it is distributed to the poor. Only when generosity replaces greed does gold find its purpose, and so we pray: *"Lord, plant in my heart the golden seeds of your word. Lead me beyond acquisition or attrition to the mystery of self-giving love that graces the world. Whenever I am tempted by monetary or spiritual avarice, return me in your mercy to the treasure of my true calling."*

4.

Manna

Exod 16:31–32. The house of Israel called it manna; it was like coriander seed, white, and the taste of it was like wafers made with honey. Moses said, "This is what the Lord has commanded: 'Let an omen of it be kept throughout your generations, in order that they may see the food with which I fed you in the wilderness, when I brought you out of the land of Egypt.'"

John 6:47–51. Very truly, I tell you, whoever believes has eternal life. I am the bread of life. Your ancestors ate the manna in the wilderness, and they died. This is the bread that comes down from heaven, so that one may eat of it and not die. I am the living bread that came down from heaven. Whoever eats of this bread will live forever; and the bread that I will give for the life of the world is my flesh.'

Whatever manna was—an edible flower, a hearty grain, a flaky wafer, a piece of unleavened bread—it saved God's people from starvation and gave them the strength to continue their desert trek. This heaven-sent food represents both a literal source of nourishment and a symbolic reminder of God's providential care. This gift from on high shatters the illusion that we can manage our own lives. Nothing could be farther from the truth. From the time of the Exodus to the present day, we are people who go about our daily existence in the hidden or overt awareness that we depend on the gracious provisions of God for our survival.

Manna does not remove the sting of our mortality, but it does make it bearable. In fact, God is always sending us one or the other sort of food in abundance. Try as we might, we will never understand the mystery behind his ways with us. The word *manna* comes from the Hebrew question, "What is it?" (Exod 16:15). We'll never know exactly, but we can surmise that it means seeing, smelling, and tasting how good is God.

The gifts lavished upon us are not parsimonious but outrageously abundant. We can come and eat at his table without paying any price. The manna he rained on the desert was both as delicious as a honey wafer and as nutritious as a whole grain cake. The people neither earned nor deserved such a relief from hunger, but that did not stop God from giving it to them. The bread that lives forever was not manna since those that ate it still died; only the bread that is the body of Jesus guarantees that we who consume it with faith will live forever (John 6:58).

Manna as a provision that comes directly from God to us remains a mystery. Something edible comes out of the ground, or ripens on a tree, or falls from a vine. Only manna comes down from the sky. Has it no roots? Does it not need fertile soil in which to grow? Rather than harvest it all at once, did the people not have to pick it fresh day by day? Such a miracle would have had to evoke awe and remind souls prone to doubt that God is faithful to them. Their cries do not go unheard. Their prayers not to perish in this wasteland are answered in the most stunning and miraculous way.

Morning after morning the manna was there. Who could doubt the majesty and mercy of God or God's desire to feed our physical and spiritual hunger? The ultimate manna sent from heaven would be his only begotten Son. Many times on our faith journey, we may feel so inwardly famined for the Holy that we do not know where to turn. We wander in a desert of aridity so lacking in consolations that God's absence appears to be more real than his presence.

Just when we least expect it, manna may be dropped upon us. It comes to us not in accordance with any agenda we have set but suddenly there it is. At one and the same time, we bow in gratitude and leap in joy. We shift from depreciative feelings of being abandoned by God to appreciative convictions that we can and must abandon ourselves to God, and so we pray: *"Lord, mellowed to the core, let me surrender to you in poverty of spirit and purity of heart. Help me once and for all to bring to an end the myth of self-sufficient power, pleasure, and possession. Reveal to me the joy of losing everything yet winning the gift of your peace in desolation and consolation. May the manna of this sublime event strengthen my faith, secure my hope, and sustain my love both now and forever."*

5.

Olives

Zech 4:1–7. The angel who talked with me came again, and wakened me, as one is wakened from sleep. He said to me, 'What do you see?' And I said, 'I see a lampstand all of gold, with a bowl on the top of it; there are seven lamps on it, with seven lips on each of the lamps that are on the top of it. And by it there are two olive trees, one on the right of the bowl and the other on its left.' I said to the angel who talked with me, 'What are these, my lord?' Then the angel who talked with me answered me, 'Do you not know what these are?' I said, 'No, my lord.' He said to me, 'This is the word of the Lord to Zerubbabel: Not by might, nor by power, but by my spirit, says the Lord of hosts. What are you, O great mountain? Before Zerubbabel you shall become a plain; and he shall bring out the top stone amid shouts of 'Grace, grace to it!'

Rom 11:17–18:24. But if some of the branches were broken off, and you, a wild olive shoot, were grafted in their place to share the rich root of the olive tree, do not vaunt yourselves over the branches. If you do vaunt yourselves, remember that it is not you that support the root, but the root that supports you. For if you have been cut from what is by nature a wild olive tree and grafted, contrary to nature, into a cultivated olive tree, how much more will these natural branches be grafted back into their own olive tree.

In the grocery store where I shop, there is a counter near the delicatessen devoted entirely to olives, green and black, ripe and cured, stuffed with blanched almonds, garlic cloves, pimento peppers, and bleu cheese. The mystery of unity in diversity lies before my grateful gaze. All are olives and yet they are small, medium, and jumbo, pitted and unpitted, soaked in vinegar or oil. I make my selection, all the while imagining how well they will compliment a Greek or Italian salad, served whole, diced or halved. They enhance almost any Mediterranean meal from pasta to chicken. Tasty as they are to eat, they can also be pressed into one of nature's richest liquids, olive oil. Better for us than butter, it ranges from light to extra virgin. Good cooks would not think of stocking their pantry without adding to it cans and bottles of this luscious commodity to which can be added herbal seasonings and other flavors.

One cannot travel in the Holy Land without seeing groves of olive trees, some of which are centuries old like those in the Garden of Gethsemane. It is even believed by some that the olive tree was the tree of life planted in the Garden of Eden. One way to care for these hearty specimens is to graft wild olive shoots on to them to replace branches that have broken off during, let us say, a violent storm. This replacement prevents one from having to tear the tree down. By the same token, a branch from an already cultivated tree can be grafted onto one that is wild to encourage the orderly growth of the olives. Entering into the heart of the mystery, the prophet Isaiah says (41:19–20): "I will put in the wilderness the cedar, the acacia, the myrtle, and the olive: I will set in the desert the cypress, the plane and the pine together, so that all may see and know, all may consider and understand, that the hand of the Lord has done this, the Holy One of Israel has created it."

New branches, like blooms in the desert, are often likened in Scripture to the Gentile believers in the first century of Christianity, who interact with the established roots of God's law of love in Judaism. The prophet Jeremiah says (11:16): "A spreading olive tree goodly to behold, the Lord has named you" and the Apostle Paul suggests that these engrafted branches can be likened to humble souls who have accepted that without the supernatural grace of God they are and can do nothing (John 15:5).

Returning to the Holy Land let us imagine for a moment how much the Lord must have enjoyed olives and their by-products at mealtime. In the world of the Bible, in the Nazareth of Jesus, Mary, and Joseph, the fruit of olive trees provided food, oil for light and heat, balm for healing. No doubt the boy picked them and watched as others pressed them into oil smooth enough to soften rough skin, pungent enough to add flavor to any ingredient. To this day, in our liturgical rites, we anoint the healthy and the sick with holy oils blessed at the Easter Vigil. It seems fitting that Jesus would undergo his final agony in an olive garden. As he would be bent under the weight of the cross, so these crooked, gnarled trees would be able in some way to absorb the blood and tears it would cost him to obey the Father's will.

At another time he may have found shade from the glaring sun under such a tree. How nice it would have been on such a day to offer him a piece of homemade bread moistened with savory olive oil, perhaps complemented with a cup of wine and a slice of cheese while we prayed: *"Lord, like sweet flowing olive oil, permeate every cell and atom of my being with your spirit of peace and joy. Fill me with the grace of knowing that the salvation of the world rests wholly in your open, wounded hands. Take my often calloused palms in yours and never let them go. Let me be like an olive tree growing in the house of God"* (Ps 52:10).

6.

Rose and Lily

Song 2:1–4.
I am a rose of Sharon,
a lily of the valleys.
As a lily among brambles,
so is my love among maidens.
As an apple tree among the trees of the wood,
so is my beloved among young men.
With great delight I sat in his shadow,
and his fruit was sweet to my taste.
He brought me to the banqueting house,
and his intention towards me was love.

Luke 12:27–28. Consider the lilies, how they grow: they neither toil nor spin; yet I tell you, even Solomon in all his glory was not clothed like one of these. But if God so clothes the grass of the field, which is alive today and tomorrow is thrown into the oven, how much more will he clothe you—you of little faith!

"Bloom where you are planted." That familiar saying echoes in the many comparisons made in scripture and in literary works between us and flowering plants like a rosebush and a lily. "She blushes like a rose." God himself "will be like dew to Israel; he shall grow like the lily, and lengthen his roots like Lebanon" (Hos 14:5). In the best of times we flourish like wildflowers, walk desert trails surrounded by spectacular blooms, or stroll with awed eyes through the beauty of a formal rose garden.

In the worst of times, the transitory nature of our life is analogous to wilted flowers in winter. We long to see the first appearance of fresh daffodils in spring, but for now all we can do is wait for a change of season. When wellbeing returns, it feels as if we are bursting like new blooms from soil freed of winter's frost. Like the roses and lilies scripture lauds, we radiate blushing beauty, whatever our age may be.

These two flowers are perhaps the most frequently mentioned ones in the Bible. The first bloom with its Easter allusions signifies the glorious profusion characteristic of spring—the tulip, the crocus, the iris, the orchid. Lilies adorn altars and graves and, like all flowers, remind us that life and death are inextricably intertwined. The rose with its thorns suggests that beauty does not rule out the possibility of brutality. Fingers that pick this flower may easily be pricked. The blood red rose is an apt description of this startling combination of cruelty and creativity. Is it not so that the crown of thorns thrust on Christ's head may have been woven from the thorny stems of rose bushes?

In her autobiography, *Story of a Soul,* Saint Thérèse of Lisieux shares a poignant experience granted to her at a young age: "Jesus deigned to teach me this mystery. He set before me the book of nature; I understood how all the flowers he has created are beautiful, how the splendor of the rose and the whiteness of the lily do not take away the perfume of the little violet or the delightful simplicity of the daisy. I understood that if all flowers wanted to be roses, nature would lose her springtime beauty, and the fields would no longer be decked out with little wild flowers."

Flowers, though themselves mute, convey voluminous words of love. That great biblical poem, the *Song of Songs,* is set in a garden that fires the senses with its scents, shapes and colors: "I am a rose of Sharon, a lily of the valleys" (Song 2:1), says the lover who pursues her lover just as the bride, the Church, seeks her bridegroom, Christ. When a husband sends his wife a dozen red roses on Valentine's Day, their perfume symbolizes the joy of a long life together. When a mother places a lily on the grave of her lost child, she conveys that the love she feels for him or her will last forever. Such is the power of flower imagery—from roses of many names and hues symbolizing life in its abundance to a single lily radiating in solitary splendor the bond that lasts beyond the sadness of death.

To compliment a person's uniqueness, we might say that she or he is like a rose among thorns or a stalwart lily surrounded by ragged weeds. A garden, no matter how well cultivated it may be, is still here today and gone tomorrow. Flowers reveal the reality of transience as well as the longing we feel for permanence. We come forth like a flower in spring and then fade away; we flee like a shadow (Job 14:2). And yet the growth that persists through every seasonal change reminds us, with or without words, that the word of God lasts forever (Isa 40:6).

Although the pride that erodes humility thinks nothing of trampling flowers under foot, God's power lets them bloom again. In the driest looking twig resides a bud waiting to blossom (Isa 35:1–2) and thereby to reveal the blessing of God's favor, the reward of undying hope, prompting us to pray: *"Lord, slow me down so I can see sunrise over spring-green gardens, roses bright and lilies white, birds feeding, bees buzzing, bushes withered by winter's cold reawakened by summer's warmth—all soaring manifestations of your wondrous creation."*

7.

Wheat and Chaff

Ps 1:4–6. The wicked are not so,
but are like chaff that the wind drives away.
Therefore the wicked will not stand in the judgment,
nor sinners in the congregation of the righteous;
for the Lord watches over the way of the righteous,
but the way of the wicked will perish.

Luke 3:16–17. John answered all of them by saying, 'I baptize you with water; but one who is more powerful than I is coming; I am not worthy to untie the thong of his sandals. He will baptize you with the Holy Spirit and fire. His winnowing-fork is in his hand, to clear his threshing-floor and to gather the wheat into his granary; but the chaff he will burn with unquenchable fire.'

In the grand scheme of life from birth to death, it is wise for us to see that the worthwhileness of wheat and the worthlessness of chaff can exist side by side. From the wheat comes the bread that is the staff of life. When one wafer of it is consecrated in the sacrament of the Eucharist, it becomes the body of Christ, consumed by believers with reverent adoration of his real presence. Such faith must steal itself against the chaff of doubt and disbelief. The life-giving kernels of Gospel-truth can be choked by the fast-multiplying weeds of falsehood. The wheat of God's grace and the chaff of illusory self-sufficiency vie for our attention; they are commingled in our fallen and redeemed souls, symbolizing the battle raging in our heart between saving virtues and depleting vices.

The functions of wheat, the value of a crop and the food it produces, all depend on a good harvest (Ps 85:12), a gift God does not withhold from his faithful people. He bestows bountiful blessings in lands that yield wheat and honey, wine and water. As Moses instructs them, the chosen people are to observe the Feast of Weeks during which they offer the first fruits of the wheat harvest to God (Exod 34:22). To feed on wheat is to acknowledge in humility that God is the one who sustains and nurtures us—who gives us our daily bread.

When God's chosen turn to idolatry, the prophet Hosea compares them to "chaff swirling from a threshing floor" (13:3). In other words, God will trample on the false gods they erect and in his mercy restore them to the stature he intended. Of Jesus John the Baptist says, "He will clear his threshing floor, gathering his wheat into the barn and burn up the chaff with unquenchable fire" (Matt 3:12).

By separating the wheat from the chaff, Jesus helps us to see what is right and good in us compared to what is wrong and evil. He knows us well enough to reveal that these two elements grow in us like the dual forces of sin and salvation. Without his help we might not be able to harvest the wheat and burn the chaff. He teaches us the art and discipline of sorting out one from the other since he wishes none of us to be lost. He is the Great Winnower, knowing precisely how to separate kernels of grain from husks of straw.

From his first public appearance at the wedding feast at Cana to the Last Supper, our Savior discloses who he is in the blessing of the wine and the breaking of the bread. Death itself has no power over him. Like leavened dough he rises again. He teaches us that to be fully alive we must sort out the chaff of selfishness from the wheat of self-giving love. Not to do so would be to forfeit our heavenly heritage like wind-swept tumbleweed (Ps 83:18).

Chaff is like smoke escaping through a window (Hos 13:3) or like straw or stubble (Exod 5:12), ready to be thrown on the fire. Over a lifetime we must let Jesus gather us like wheat into the barn of the Church he built, praying in the process: *"Lord, already the fields are ripe for the harvest. Let me be among the laborers you choose to gather souls into the granary of your spirit. Separate the golden grain of their graced destiny from the straw of attachment that all may sing about the mystery they most deeply are."*

PART THREE

Things Invested with Transcendent Meaning

1.

Bones

Ps 34:19–22. Many are the afflictions of the righteous,
but the Lord rescues them from them all.
He keeps all their bones;
not one of them will be broken.
Evil brings death to the wicked,
and those who hate the righteous will be condemned.
The Lord redeems the life of his servants;
none of those who take refuge in him will be condemned.

John 19:32–36. Then the soldiers came and broke the
legs of the first and of the other who had been crucified
with him. But when they came to Jesus and saw that he
was already dead, they did not break his legs. Instead,
one of the soldiers pierced his side with a spear, and at
once blood and water came out. (He who saw this has
testified so that you also may believe. His testimony is
true, and he knows that he tells the truth.) These things
occurred so that the scripture might be fulfilled, 'None of
his bones shall be broken.'

When flesh has long since turned to dust bones remain, intact and
full of forensic evidence, a source of fascination for paleontologists.

Future physicians study skeletal bones in anatomy classes. Museums collect them in their halls of natural history; cold case experts piece them together to ascertain the method and time of a victim's demise. In the Bible, bones point to the physical and spiritual essence of a person since they are the only evidence left of his or her existence (Job 20:11 and 30:17). One is awed by the fact that into the seemingly inert matter that makes up bones God breathes his spirit (Eccl 11:15).

Bones describe many facets of our personhood as when we say we experience aches in all our bones (anguish) or feel under the weight of sin that every bone in our body is broken. In the First Book of Kings (13:31) and in the Second (13:21), a lifeless body, upon touching Elisha's bones, receives its spirit and stands upright. In Ezekiel's Valley of Dry Bones, a field strewn with skeletal remains regains flesh and comes to life again (Ezek 37), revealing that nothing is impossible for God.

When Adam sees Eve in the Garden of Eden, he recognizes their oneness by calling her "bone of my bones" (Gen 2:23). Bones not only preserve our original essence; they also resist the normal process of decay. Whereas the bones of the wicked lie "strewn at the mouth of Sheol" (Ps 141:7), those of the just are rejoined to the body on the last day. So precious are the bones of Jesus Christ that on the cross a prophecy comes true, for not one of his bones were broken (John 19:33–36; Ps 34:20).

Surely what happened to Christ stands as a reminder of the Passover regulations that prohibited breaking the bones of the sacrificial lamb (Exod 12:46; Num 9:12). The patriarchs before Jesus made sure that their bones would come to rest in the Promised Land. This was Joseph's wish (Exod 13:19). Unburied bones defiled the land (Ezekiel 39:15) and contact with them desecrated the altar (Ezek 6:5).

In a non-biblical context, tribal peoples, especially Shamans, collect bones from various creatures and rattle them over the sick in a healing ritual. Perhaps because bones last over eons of time they are thought to be invested with sacred powers. Terminally ill people appear at times so frail that one can see their bones through their skin. After death, the shape of a skull shows archeologists where a species fits in the evolutionary chain of life. Bones age while remaining remarkably ageless. They signal our finitude but not without reference to our hope for immortality. The bones of saints are invested with such a profound religions meaning that they become relics. Bones like these are for believers' tangible pointers to persons of holiness whose walk on earth led them to heaven.

Most people at one time or another have had a broken bone—a wrist, a leg, an elbow, a hip. The beauty is that bones can be welded back together, restitched and replaced, thereby manifesting the remarkable versatility of God's creation, and so we pray: *"Lord, teach me not to cling to what is gone when life invites me to move on. I am to be both an explorer and a restorer, a person who sees new life emerging from the old as years that swiftly come as swiftly go."*

2.

Books

Ps 69:27–29. Add guilt to their guilt;
may they have no acquittal from you.
Let them be blotted out of the book of the living;
let them not be enrolled among the righteous.
But I am lowly and in pain;
let your salvation, O God, protect me.

Rev 21:23–27. And the city has no need of sun or moon
to shine on it, for the glory of God is its light, and its
lamp is the Lamb. The nations will walk by its light, and
the kings of the earth will bring their glory into it. Its
gates will never be shut by day—and there will be no
night there. People will bring into it the glory and the
honor of the nations. But nothing unclean will enter it,
nor anyone who practices abomination or falsehood, but
only those who are written in the Lamb's book of life.

Books are treasures most people love and targets a few of them
hate like the book-burning hordes unleashed by the Nazi regime
at the start of the Second World War. It would be hard to find
anyone who does not own a book, a scroll, a parchment or some

other material inscribed with a text. Books line library shelves where readers browse for hours, admiring their binding, size, and shape—qualities not replicated on a computer screen. There is no substitute for holding a book in one's hand and marking an owned copy. No one has to prove to parents that reading to their children readies them in the best possible way for their further education.

In the "book of life" there is written the time of our birth and the date of our death. We believers live in the light of God's revealed word in the Bible. Truths that have inspired and guided humankind have been chiseled on tablets of stone or inscribed on animal skins, wound tight and rolled to form a scroll. Three thousand years before Christ, writing was done in Egypt on rolls of papyrus, the same material on which the Jews recorded the Law of Moses. There are over a hundred references in the Bible to the Book of the Law and the Book of the Covenant.

In that mystical heavenly book are inscribed the names and deeds of those destined to dwell in the eternal city (Rev 20:15). In Psalm 139:6 we read with wonder the events written by God in the book of our life "before one of them came to be." The prophet Ezekiel is told to eat a sacred scroll to signify his complete adherence to the will of God and his obedience to God's call: "So I ate it, and it tasted as sweet as honey in my mouth" (3:3).

The power of the word is such that it can be and is a source of conversion. One day in a garden, Augustine of Hippo heard the voice of a child saying, "Take and read." Immediately, he turned to a Bible lying on a nearby table and opened it to Paul's letter to the Romans. There he experienced in God's word the divine directive he most needed to hear. He was told to stop his carousing and to put on the Lord, Jesus Christ (Rom 13:14). Without any hesitation that is what he did.

Our Savior himself was a lover of the word. He is depicted time and again unfolding a scroll and interpreting its meaning. We, too, are to read the words he gave us not only for the information (Divine Revelation) they contain but also for the inner transformation of heart they evoke. While the Bible is a collection of many books, it is really a singularly sacred work that invites us to believe that God is with us, that God's plan is to save us, and that in the end good will triumph over evil.

Books beyond the Bible have become literary classics and spiritual treasures. These jewels take many forms—poetry and prose, essays and novels, collections of letters and edifying journals. In them we meet heroes and heroines. We find friends near and far who understand our feelings, share our ideas, and inspire us to make bold and passionate moves in intellectual, social, and religious life.

Books frighten and console, stir up revolutions and record the lives of saints. The author may be long gone, but his or her words continue to live in the minds of readers. What we imbibe in a good book is as vital to our spirit as food is to our body, and so we pray: *"Lord, more important to me than what I consume at table is the truth that I have been called forth from eternity to be a unique epiphany of your mystery. Turn my life, humble as it may be, into an open book of faith, hope, and love available for all to read."*

3.

Cups

Ps 23:5–6. You prepare a table before me
in the presence of my enemies;
you anoint my head with oil;
my cup overflows.
Surely goodness and mercy shall follow me
all the days of my life,
and I shall dwell in the house of the Lord
my whole life long.

I Cor 11:23–26. For I received from the Lord what I also
handed on to you, that the Lord Jesus on the night when
he was betrayed took a loaf of bread, and when he had
given thanks, he broke it and said, 'This is my body that is
for you. Do this in remembrance of me.' In the same way
he took the cup also, after supper, saying, 'This cup is the
new covenant in my blood. Do this, as often as you drink
it, in remembrance of me.' For as often as you eat this
bread and drink the cup, you proclaim the Lord's death
until he comes.

Cups in and by themselves are rather innocuous vessels. Neigh-
bors knock on one another's doors to borrow a cup of sugar. In the

morning we enjoy a steaming cup of coffee or tea. Sports figures standing in the winner's circle proudly hold up a sailing, hockey, or racing cup. In the desert a cup of water can mean the difference between life or death.

Cups come in all shapes and sizes, but what gives them their significance is not how they look or of what material (silver or ceramic) they are made but the significance of what they contain. Does the liquid within slake thirst or does it contribute to drunkenness and in the worst of cases death? The blessing or curse contained in a pewter cup is no different from what one might put in a wooden vessel full of water or poison.

Cups can also tell us a story. Tin ones hanging on rusty wall hooks remind us of the Old West. We may trace the service of a royal family to the china cups they collected. Jesus commends the kindness of anyone who will give his disciples a cup of cold water (Matt 10:42). We know from his own life that when we have to drink from the cup of suffering, our only recourse may be to swallow it to the last dregs and trust that a new day will come.

Blessing cups symbolize all the benefits and favors God provides, such as in Psalm 23:5 which says, "My cup overflows." The opposite occurs when God, the Divine Judge, has to give the wicked a cup of wrath drawing them into a drunken stupor and possibly dying in rebellion because they refused to repent. As God tells the nations, "Drink, get drunk and vomit, and fall to rise no more" (Jer 25:27).

Arrogance tricks alcoholics into thinking they can hold their liquor, but instead it may cause them to lose their dignity and end up in a gutter, with no bragging rights left (Hab 2:16). Some go mad (Jer 51:7); others are scorned and stepped upon by their foes (Isa 51:23). God's anger is not to blame. This devastation happens by virtue of their irresponsible choices.

This vessel can also signify a flood of divine grace as when Jesus prays in the Garden of Gethsemane, "Abba Father . . . take this cup from me" (Mark 14:36) and in the same breath chooses to surrender to the plan of the Father for him. As the soldiers come to arrest him, he says with a beautiful blending of humility and heroic virtue, "Shall I not drink the cup the Father has given me?" (John 18:11).

The cup of the new covenant is filled with the wine of Christ's blood that he wants followers to drink for the forgiveness of sins (Matt 26:27–29). He assures us that what flows from this cup is the grace of life eternal (I Cor 11:25–26.) Once consumed with compunction this blessed drink marks the start of the new covenant between him and us.

In an artifact shop in Jerusalem, I found a vessel called a "tear cup." It was to be placed directly under one's eyes to catch, as it were, the waters of repentance. The gift of tears often happens when we accept the saving power of the Lord in our sinful lives. Reconciled to him, we approach the Eucharistic table where ordinary altar wine consecrated in the chalice becomes the blood of Christ. The sharing of the cup is a sign of our oneness in the faith community. Like mugs of cheer passed around a Christmas table, the blessing cup makes us feel at home with ourselves, others, and God, and so we pray: *"Lord, you see me at my best and worst, caught between defiance and docility, and still you treat me to the intoxicating wine of love divine. Awe for your mystery sweeps me away. Despite my love of words, there is less and less for me to say."*

4.

Gates

Deut 6:4–9. Hear, O Israel: The Lord is our God, the Lord alone. You shall love the Lord your God with all your heart, and with all your soul, and with all your might. Keep these words that I am commanding you today in your heart. Recite them to your children and talk about them when you are at home and when you are away, when you lie down and when you rise. Bind them as a sign on your hand, fix them as an emblem on your fore-head, and write them on the doorposts of your house and on your gates.

Matt 16:15–18. He said to them, 'But who do you say that I am?' Simon Peter answered, 'You are the Messiah, the Son of the living God.' And Jesus answered him, 'Blessed are you, Simon son of Jonah! For flesh and blood has not revealed this to you, but my Father in heaven. And I tell you, you are Peter, and on this rock I will build my church, and the gates of Hades will not prevail against it.'

Across the spectrum of daily life, gates have a double meaning. In some cases they are entry ways, let us say, to a garden or a building complex. In other cases, they prevent us from passing from one place to another as when the gates of a prison slam behind a criminal. In a walled city like Jerusalem, gates are given names and special meanings like the Sheep Gate or the Fish Gate or the Horse Gate (Neh 3:1–28) where perhaps these goods were sold. People push through gates and dislike it when they close. Fortified gates provide good defenses. Garden gates welcome visitors. However massive gates may be, no fortress is impenetrable.

Artists can spend their precious time decorating gates or they can be installed at a moment's notice. In the olden days city gates were shut at night for protection and opened in the morning to encourage commerce. Breaching gates made of bronze was no easy endeavor whereas wooden ones could be set aflame. To be a gate-keeper was a duty and an honor (2 Kgs 10, 11, 12), for if the gate failed the whole city could fall with it. Gates were natural gathering places. In the Book of Proverbs, Wisdom places herself at the entrance of the city gates (Prov 1:21). Markets flourished near them; beggars sat before them. In their vicinity legal negotiations were carried on and sometimes the reward or punishment that followed was meted out (Deut 17:5.)

References to gates in the bible are not only literal but figurative. As we read in Psalm 87:2, "The Lord loves the gates of Zion more than all the dwellings of Jacob." It is through the Golden Gates that the King of glory will enter (Ps 24:7). The church, the Bride of Christ, is so favored by the Father that the gates of Hell will not prevail against her (Matt 16:18). Who of us, judged pleasing to God would not want to enter the pearly gates of heaven? Jesus used the image of the "narrow gate" to remind us that it is difficult to obey the laws that lead to paradise whereas the wide gate that welcomes evildoers leads to perdition. How impressive it is to hear Jesus call himself the safest gate of all. He says, "I am the gate. Whoever enters by me will be saved" (John 10:9).

As our life unfolds, we must choose with care what gates we pass through. The poet Dante, author of *The Divine Comedy*, warns anyone who crosses the gates that demarcate the Inferno to abandon all hope. No wonder survivors of the holocaust felt exactly this way when the gates of hell in the concentration camps closed them off from the civilized world. How tempting it must have been for them to shut the gates of their heart and to refuse to trust anyone ever again. Under such circumstances could one still cling to the prophecy that the gates of the New Jerusalem "will never be shut by day—and there will be no night there" (Rev 21: 25)?

Walking along a strange road, we may come upon a gate. We hesitate to open it because we do not know what lies on the other side. Do we turn around and proceed safely along the road on which we came or do we unlatch the gate, walk through it, and explore what lies beyond? Jesus, the gateway to the Trinity, tells us not to fear the adventure of faith. He wants to lead us to the unknown land where love abounds, and so we pray, *"Lord, let the brightness of your glory radiate around the eternal gates through which I one day hope to pass. Let me join the heavenly hosts in their song of everlasting praise. May my life bear fruit in your own good time despite my countless failures."*

5.

Stones

Josh 4:5–7. Joshua said to them, 'Pass on before the ark of the Lord your God into the middle of the Jordan, and each of you take up a stone on his shoulder, one for each of the tribes of the Israelites, so that this may be a sign among you. When your children ask in time to come, "What do those stones mean to you?" then you shall tell them that the waters of the Jordan were cut off in front of the ark of the covenant of the Lord. When it crossed over the Jordan, the waters of the Jordan were cut off. So these stones shall be to the Israelites a memorial for ever.'

I Pet 2:4–7. Come to him, a living stone, though rejected by mortals yet chosen and precious in God's sight, and like living stones, let yourselves be built into a spiritual house, to be a holy priesthood, to offer spiritual sacrifices acceptable to God through Jesus Christ. For it stands in scripture:

'See, I am laying in Zion a stone,
a cornerstone chosen and precious;
and whoever believes in him will not be put to shame.'
To you then who believe, he is precious; but for those who do not believe,
'The stone that the builders rejected
has become the very head of the corner' . . .

That "sing-song" of our youthful days, "Sticks and stones can hurt my bones, but names can never harm me" is a lie. Names can destroy a person's confidence as much as sharp-edged stones can scar unprotected skin. Stones may be inert objects, lifeless and opaque, but their consequences are not. Good farmers can gather them to build protective fences around their crops. Vengeful militants can make of them weapons of destruction. The Ten Commandments were carved by the finger of God on tablets of stone and Moses saw them as life-giving elements (Deut 4:13). Stones serve as silent witnesses to God's truths (Gen 31:44–54); as images of hard, unresponsive hearts that must be renewed (Ezek 36:26); and as symbols of the endurance of God's kingdom and of God himself as the rock of ages (Gen 49:24.)

Stones can vindicate God's cause as when the shepherd boy David put a smooth stone in his slingshot and slew the giant Goliath (I Sam 17;21:9). In the wilderness, hungry as he might have been, Jesus resisted Satan's temptation to turn stones to bread (Luke 4:4). Stones can betray God's will to forgive as when a crowd of hypocrites picked them up with the intention of killing the woman caught in adultery (John 8:3). Jesus once told his disciples that there were times when he had to use a stone for a pillow because he had no other place on which to lay his head (Matt 8:20). Yet the stone rejected by the builders would become the cornerstone upholding the world, the Church, and every sincerely seeking soul (Eph 2:20).

Christ is the "living stone" (I Pet 2:4) that no force on earth or under the earth can crush. In Ephesians 2:20–21, Paul sees the church stretching far and wide "built upon the foundation of the apostles and prophets with Christ Jesus himself as the cornerstone. In him the whole structure is joined together and grows into a holy temple in the Lord."

All of these allusions and revelations remind us how precious stones can be. We recall that rare gemstones—emeralds, sapphires,

diamonds—are often more valuable than currency. Stone formations tell the story of ancient burial sites whose ritual meaning has
to be mined by every generation. What to the untrained eye looks
like a pile of rubble may be a collection of priceless artifacts. The
solidity of stone preserves their story. That is why we choose them
as the building blocks of our houses and churches.

Spires point to the heavens. Dams enable rushing water to
turn into electrical power. Slabs of marble become great works
of art under the chisels of a master stone-carver. Stones rubbed
smooth or crafted into prayer beads can pass through our fingers
and bring us comfort. Weapons once used to kill one's foes can be
hurled into a hot furnace until they melt like wax. Guns rendered
inert line hallowed walls and give glory to God for whose mercy
we pray: *"Lord, let these silent sentinels teach me to cease fighting
bloody battles and foster your peace. Let me stand in wordless wonder beholding the way in which slabs of stone have been recrafted
into church steeples honoring your revelation manifested in the
bricks and mortar of a splendid human creation."*

6.

Temples

I Macc 4:47–51. Then they took unhewn stones, as the law directs, and built a new altar like the former one. They also rebuilt the sanctuary and the interior of the temple, and consecrated the courts. They made new holy vessels, and brought the lampstand, the altar of incense, and the table into the temple. Then they offered incense on the altar and lit the lamps on the lampstand, and these gave light in the temple. They placed the bread on the table and hung up the curtains. Thus they finished all the work they had undertaken.

I Cor 3:16–17. Do you not know that you are God's temple and that God's Spirit dwells in you? If anyone destroys God's temple, God will destroy that person. For God's temple is holy, and you are that temple.

Temple mounds, considered sacred sites, adorn the geography of Mayans and Romans, Jews and Greeks whose belief systems differ but whose awesome edifices are said to be the dwelling place of God and of the gods for polytheistic religions. From ancient ruins to gleaming visions of modern Mormon and Masonic temples, these grand structures are both objects of exploration and architectural masterpieces that to the naked eye defy description.

In the Hebrew scriptures no place is more honored than the temple of Solomon, the worship center of the Jewish religion, crafted to the exact specifications revealed by the Master Architect. This sanctuary, this house of God, is the divine habitation where heaven intersects earth (Ps 132:13).

Whereas pagan temples might be adorned from one end to the other with personifications of gods and goddesses, Solomon's temple emphasized the sobriety, the sovereignty, the permanence of the one true God. Precious metals like gold were used to symbolize the glory of the Lord just as massive stone pillars marked the entrance to his abode. A tent might blow away in the wind but a temple seemed destined to stand for ages to come. Here the people could feel blessed and protected by God, knowing that the Most High had chosen this place in which to dwell while not being confined within its walls. The temple symbolized the paradox of God's coming among us while being far beyond us (I Kgs 8:27): "The Lord is in his holy temple; the Lord's throne is in heaven" (Ps 11:4). May we rest in peace in this place from the beginning to the end of our life.

The majesty of the temple matched the mystery of God's victory over foes bent on destroying the faith and fortune of the chosen people. David's son Solomon built the temple to celebrate God's might and to show the complementarity between the celestial and the terrestrial abodes of God. Here is a stunning revelation of God in creation and a magnificent edifice built by human hands. The light of creation (Gen 1:3) flows into the light of the tabernacle (Exod 40:34) and both lights shine in the temple (2 Chr 2:12). Symbolic of the seven days of creation, the temple of Solomon took seven years to build. God himself was its chief contractor. Here was the place where God spoke to those with ears to hear like Simeon and Anna. Yet despite its glory the temple of Solomon did not stand. Whereas stone and glass are subject to destruction, not even a death as cruel as crucifixion could prevent the Lord from rising again on the third day. Vows made in temple precincts by unscrupulous types could be broken, but Christ's promises stand firm forever. He is the living temple who dwells among us.

In a similar vein, each baptized person is a temple in which the Lord takes up his abode. The sacrifice that pleases him is not the blood of goats or bulls but the living flame of love that burns in our hearts. Each time we cross the threshold from secular to sacred space, walk down the aisle of the church, and approach the Tabernacle that houses the consecrated host that is the body of Christ, we realize what being in God's temple means, and so we pray: *"Lord, protect me from the temptation to defile the temple of my spirit, heart, mind, and will. Keep me holy as you are holy and restore in me the hope of immortality. Let me be an epiphany of your presence wherever you place me and grant that false gods may never stand between me and your singular majesty."*

7.

Thrones

Isa 6:1–3. In the year that King Uzziah died, I saw the Lord sitting on a throne, high and lofty; and the hem of his robe filled the temple. Seraphs were in attendance above him; each had six wings: with two they covered their faces, and with two they covered their feet, and with two they flew. And one called to another and said: 'Holy, holy, holy is the Lord of hosts; the whole earth is full of his glory.'

Matt 19:27–30. Then Peter said in reply, 'Look, we have left everything and followed you. What then will we have?' Jesus said to them, 'Truly I tell you, at the renewal of all things, when the Son of Man is seated on the throne of his glory, you who have followed me will also sit on twelve thrones, judging the twelve tribes of Israel. And everyone who has left houses or brothers or sisters or father or mother or children or fields, for my name's sake, will receive a hundredfold, and will inherit eternal life. But many who are first will be last, and the last will be first.'

Thrones in all civilizations are symbols of power and might. On them sit rulers who spread wisdom and peace as well as tyrants who commit dreadful crimes from unmitigated greed to genocide. The throne on which sits the Risen Christ signifies glory, splendor, majesty, victory, and eternal benevolence to all who sing, "Holy, holy, holy, Lord." To bow before God's throne is to acknowledge in humility God's sovereignty over us. It is to say from the depths of our heart, "I am nothing; you are all!" Our king is Jesus the Christ. In his kingdom evil can gain no permanent foothold. Mary, Queen of Heaven, is often pictured on a bejeweled throne. She shows us with dignity and grace that in God's reign the lowly are lifted high and that from time immemorial all will call her blessed.

The thrones of earthly kings, however powerful they appear to be, are destined to be ground to dust. Neither pharaoh nor all his chariots could stand up against the might of God (Exod 11:5; 12:29). Human thrones can be reminiscent of righteousness and wise judgment, as was Solomon's throne (I Kgs 2:19; 10:18), but on them can also sit evil men like Nero, playing his fiddle while Rome burned.

Artifacts of thrones may tell the story of a dynasty that thought it was too powerful to fall. Now they lie in ruins while we who observe them are drawn to ask the perennial question, "At what price glory?" Such thrones create a chasm between master and slave. By contrast, the throne of David from whose house would come the Savior of the world, was a symbol of divine promise, meaning that David and his descendants would rule Israel in perpetuity—a prophecy communicated to David by Nathan (I Sam 7) and fulfilled in Jesus Christ (Matt 1:1; Luke 1:32), who would make his throne accessible to all believers.

The more we bow to the Lord, the more he meets our gaze with infinite mercy, reminding us of the paradox that the exalted are humbled and the humble exalted.

Surrounding the throne of Christ the King is a crystal-clear sea of glass (Rev 4:6) and countless hosts of angels (Rev 5:11), a sight more awesome than any of us can imagine. From this dazzlingly white throne (Rev 20:11) flows a "river of living water" (Rev

22:1). No corrupt throne (Ps 94:20), neither the royal one of Babylon (Isa 14:13) nor that of Satan (Rev 2:13), can stand up against this one. They have no staying power compared to the splendor of God's throne pictured in all its glory in the Book of Revelation, which describes God's final victory over Satan and the forces of evil.

While on earth Christ rejected every outward sign of power. In becoming powerless he exuded the only power strong enough to pulverize the Prince of this world. We may picture him as a boy in Nazareth, sitting on a wooden chair, built perhaps by Joseph, the carpenter, of the same material on which he would one day be crucified for our redemption. We may see him on a royal throne seated at the right hand of the Father. In either case, our happiest posture is to sit at his feet and pray: *"Lord, let no hidden hostility disguise itself as zeal for your kingdom. Help me to transfigure a world peopled by those who resist your word into a land of love that allows souls readied by grace to be benefactors of your blessing."*

PART FOUR

Places in Nature Pointing to God

1.

Clouds

Dan 7:13–14. As I watched in the night visions,
I saw one like a human being
coming with the clouds of heaven.
And he came to the Ancient One
and was presented before him.
To him was given dominion
and glory and kingship,
that all peoples, nations, and languages
should serve him.
His dominion is an everlasting dominion
that shall not pass away,
and his kingship is one
that shall never be destroyed.

Luke 21:25–28. 'There will be signs in the sun, the moon,
and the stars, and on the earth distress among nations
confused by the roaring of the sea and the waves. People
will faint from fear and foreboding of what is coming
upon the world, for the powers of the heavens will be
shaken. Then they will see "the Son of Man coming in
a cloud" with power and great glory. Now when these
things begin to take place, stand up and raise your heads,
because your redemption is drawing near.'

In the following poem, I try to express a few of the myriad meanings we may attribute to these ever changing formations that fill the sky from horizon to horizon:

> Clouds,
> hung like sheets to dry,
> evoke hushed waves of wonder,
> sunder foolish illusions
> of human pride and power,
> winsome reminders of our lack of control.
>
> Clouds,
> unfold in shapely splendor,
> reminding us that neither nature's
> fury nor its fruition
> can be taken for granted—
> all that is depends on divine compassion.
>
> Clouds,
> transform themselves moment by moment,
> compelling us to commemorate anew
> the mystery that embraces,
> Mother Earth, drawing us
> towards an ecstasy of love beyond all telling.

Who of us has not laid prone in a field of grass, looking up and watching the clouds go by? There's a train, a boat, a rabbit, a wise old owl! Suddenly storm clouds gather on the horizon, forecasting a change in the weather. We head for home, wondering what will come—a much needed summer shower or pelting rain that will drive us indoors.

Clouds appearing in the Bible seldom carry these meteorological connotations. True, clouds rising from the sea might mean rain (I Kgs 18:44) while those scattered in high cirrus formations were most likely rainless (Jude 12). Clouds could also connote the mystery of God's guiding hand. After their exodus from Egypt, the Israelites' journey across the desert was marked by a pillar of cloud by day and one of fire by night (Exod 13:21; 14:19). The glory of the Lord was so radiant (Rev 1:16) that he had to hide himself behind a cloud since no one on earth could see God's face and live. That is why a thick cloud covered Mount Sinai when God revealed his law to Moses (Exod 19:16). Later, when Israel sinned and turned against God, the Holy departed from them in a cloud (Ezek 10:3–4). It was a cloud that carried the warrior God away in a chariot (Isa 19:1–2) and a cloud that revealed the light of grace from which sin could not hide (Isa 44:22). In the New Testament, at the transfiguration on Mount Tabor, the Father spoke out of a cloud and blessed his chosen Son (Luke 9:35).

In the fourteenth-century classic, *The Cloud of Unknowing*, the anonymous author uses this formation metaphorically to point to the unknowability of the Transcendent. He says that thought knocks at the door of this cloud hiding the mystery but only love enters. The author further advises that we ought to press our tendency to dwell on our faults and failings under a "cloud of forgetting." God in his mercy forgives our mistakes and harbors no memory of them, so why should we?

At times when the solution to a pressing problem evades us, we say that our mind feels cloudy. When something unpleasant happens to us, we hold to the hope that in every cloud there is a silver lining. Flying from one city to another, we await the thrilling moment when our jet pierces above the ceiling of clouds and we see the sun. When clouds hang low over the earth we cannot see the hand in front of us, so thick is the fog they create. Innocent as they may look from a distance, clouds can gather strength and produce ferocious storms of hurricane force. High in the sky they look beautiful, but they can change course in seconds as storm-chasers testify. Our life, too, can be clear or cloudy, following a sure course of action or deterred by doubt and ambiguity. The hope we harbor for clarity becomes invested in Jesus Christ. When the Son of God returns to us his chariot will burst through the clouds (Rev 1:7) and our joy will be complete. Greeting him we pray, *"Lord, even though my life passes as fast as clouds scattered on a windy day I believe that you are with me always. No storm can change your course of salvation or hide your intention to bring me to the eternal homeland for which I long on the clearest or cloudiest day."*

2.

Mountains

Isa 40:3–5. A voice cries out:
'In the wilderness prepare the way of the Lord,
make straight in the desert a highway for our God.
Every valley shall be lifted up,
and every mountain and hill be made low;
the uneven ground shall become level,
and the rough places a plain.
Then the glory of the Lord shall be revealed,
and all people shall see it together,
for the mouth of the Lord has spoken.'

Matt 5:14–16. 'You are the light of the world. A city built on a hill cannot be hidden. No one after lighting a lamp puts it under the bushel basket, but on the lampstand, and it gives light to all in the house. In the same way, let your light shine before others, so that they may see your good works and give glory to your Father in heaven.'

Who of us could forget the scene in *The Sound of Music* when Julie Andrews comes into view with the Alps in the background and sings with joy, "The hills are alive with the sound of music," and it is as if we can hear it, too. Biblical landscapes are also alive with hills and mountains. Their geographical significance ranges from providing a refuge from foes to contributing to the strategy to slay them. They are places that command the worship of God and barriers demarcating one nation from another. Some look barren and lifeless, others are lush.

One of the reasons I love living in Western Pennsylvania is because the terrain unfolds in a series of rolling hills that one can climb to enjoy spectacular views. Even an amateur hiker can scale beginners' trails in the Blue Ridge Mountains or explore the Laurel Caverns and their intriguing rock and crystal formations. With a little imagination, we can think of Jesus walking around the hill country, pausing for prayer, and then choosing a mount on which to proclaim his beatitudes (Matt 5). Such sublime pronouncements seem to require as an ideal setting a high place.

In his farewell blessing to Israel, Moses, who along with Elijah Jesus met on Mount Tabor, speaks poetically of "ancient mountains . . . and everlasting hills" (Deut 33:15). Mountains can be as formidable as they are beautiful, tumbling over in an earthquake or erupting during a volcano. They are often depicted as symbols of God's power since "the mountains melt like wax before the Lord" (Ps 97:5). Jesus assures us that if we have faith we can cast mountains into the sea (Matt 17:20) and put problems in their place by remembering not to make a mountain out of a molehill!

Even flying over the Alps, let alone climbing up them or skiing down them, is evocative of pure awe. Surely God is in this place as when Moses heard him speak from the bush alight with fire that did not burn on "Horeb, the Mountain of God" (Exod 3:1–2) or when the prophet ascended Mount Sinai to meet the mystery face to face (Exod 19). Jesus went to such places to enjoy solitary prayer (Luke 6:12), and it was on a mountain that he found the strength to refute Satan and resist his temptations (Matt 4:8; Luke 4:5). Jesus died on Calvary and after the resurrection ascended to heaven from the Mount of Olives (Acts 1:10–12).

Mystics like Francis of Assisi climbed mountains like that of Alvernia in Umbria where he received the stigmata of the Lord.

Mountains seem to be perfect settings for such epiphanic mani-festations. In the monastic tradition the ideal location for a mon-astery is a place like Monte Cassino where the first followers of Saint Benedict found the silence and solitude they craved. It is not surprising that mountains and mountainous imagery fill the pro-phetic books of the Bible (Isaiah, Jeremiah, Ezekiel, and the Book of Revelation).

On the road of life, when we are lost, we often find our bear-ings by climbing to a higher place and surveying the land around us. Then we decide what road to take. All by all, mountains and hills help us to find our destination. On them we witness a cornu-copia of human activity—from hiding to fighting, from getting our bearings to encountering our Beloved to whom we pray: *"Lord, lend me a voice by which to sing your praises from on high. Let me laud you as the King of glory who leapt like a fierce warrior into the doomed land and chose to house yourself in the lowliness of my seeking and sinful soul."*

3.

Morning

Lam 3:22–24.
The steadfast love of the Lord never ceases,
his mercies never come to an end;
they are new every morning;
great is your faithfulness.
'The Lord is my portion,' says my soul,
'therefore I will hope in him.'

2 Pet 1:19–21. So we have the prophetic message more fully confirmed. You will do well to be attentive to this as to a lamp shining in a dark place, until the day dawns and the morning star rises in your hearts. First of all you must understand this, that no prophecy of scripture is a matter of one's own interpretation, because no prophecy ever came by human will, but men and women moved by the Holy Spirit spoke from God.

Morning dawns and with it a new day. Though it may be dark in another part of the world, on the horizon we see a blush of orange, a touch of red, signaling that however difficult yesterday was, today we can make a fresh start. Certain mornings, like birthdays and

Christmas, are special but for Christians no dawning can rival the splendor of Easter morning with its heartwarming greeting, "My joy! Christ is risen from the dead, risen as he truly said. Alleluia!"

Aware of his presence, we sense anew why we must pursue God's plan for our life. Carried on the wings of the dawn (Ps 139:9), we feel rejuvenated. After several days without sun we feel almost rapturous when its warmth shines on our face. Many people, myself included, call themselves morning persons. Glorious as a sunset can be, nothing rivals sunrise. I seldom, if ever, need an alarm clock to get me out of bed. At first light, I'm up and at it—time for prayer, for spiritual reading, for journaling, all jump-starting the creative ideas born in the morning and growing throughout the day.

There is a great contrast in the literature of spirituality between the light of day and the darkness of night. For the Divine there is no such boundary, but in truth daylight militates against deeds committed in the dark (Judg 19:25). The manna showered on the desert at night had to be eaten before the following morning lest it became inedible (Exod 16:19–24). In another vein armies do battle in the morning (2 Chr 20:20) and recover their strength afterwards in sleep. It was "early in the morning" that Abraham set out under obedience to sacrifice his son Isaac (Gen 22:3), and, after Jacob wrestled with the angel and received a new name (Gen 32:31), the sun rose and the day began with prayer and worship as its centerpiece. Every morning signifies anew the outpouring of God's faithfulness and steadfast love (Lam 3:23).

The morning enables a disappointing as well as a good discovery, for only then did Jacob see that he had married the wrong woman (Gen 29:25). Another found her infant son dead in the morning (I Kings 3:21) and in the morning light God revealed to Abraham the destruction of Sodom (Gen 19:27). Nothing of our deeds falls outside of God's gaze, for every morning [the Lord] renders his judgment (Zeph 3:5). Was it not at dawn that the Red Sea returned to its normal depth, swallowing the Egyptian charioteers in pursuit of the Chosen People (Exod 14:27). The greatest exodus of all—that of Jesus from the tomb—happened in the morning (Matt 28:1), offering us lasting hope and sealing the faith to which we now adhere.

It is inspiring to imagine Jesus yawning and stretchy after a good night's sleep and at first light looking heavenward in praise of the Father. We appeal to him at the same time of day, saying, "Lord, in the morning you hear my voice; in the morning I plead my case to you" (Ps 5:3). In the night, we weep; in the morning we rejoice (Ps 30:5). We equate Christ himself with the "bright morning star" (Rev 22:16). We hear the Apostle Peter exhort us to listen to God's word "until the day dawns and the morning star rises in [our] hearts (2 Pet 1:19).

Fresh thoughts, new hopes, beneficial energy—all are morning gifts, and so we pray, *"Lord, continue to build a bridge between my nothingness and your allness. Amidst stark aridity, may there shine forth the bright light of your presence. Remind me when my courage ebbs not to lose heart. Take away the fear I feel when I realize I must make a fresh start. Raise my eyes to behold with grateful wonder the morning light peeking over the horizon and teaching me the age-old lesson that in every ending there is a new beginning."*

4.

Night

Exod 13:21–22. The Lord went in front of them in a pillar of cloud by day, to lead them along the way, and in a pillar of fire by night, to give them light, so that they might travel by day and by night. Neither the pillar of cloud by day nor the pillar of fire by night left its place in front of the people.

I Thess 5:4–11. But you, beloved, are not in darkness, for that day to surprise you like a thief; for you are all children of light and children of the day; we are not of the night or of darkness. So then, let us not fall asleep as others do, but let us keep awake and be sober; for those who sleep at night, and those who are drunk get drunk at night. But since we belong to the day, let us be sober, and put on the breastplate of faith and love, and for a helmet the hope of salvation. For God has destined us not for wrath but for obtaining salvation through our Lord Jesus Christ, who died for us, so that whether we are awake or asleep we may live with him. Therefore encourage one another and build up each other, as indeed you are doing.

Emotions like panic, fear, doubt, and anxiety may rise up at night-fall. As Psalm 30 reminds us: "At nightfall, weeping enters in, but with the dawn rejoicing." When intellect, memory, and will are at their weakest, during what Saint John of the Cross names the "dark night of the soul," we have only one option: to cling to Father, Son and Holy Spirit in naked faith, undaunted hope, and unconditional love. The only way to break out of these midnight moments is, with the help of grace, to break through them.

Both night and day point to the beauty, mystery, and magnitude of creation. In nature many species thrive at night and return to their burrows by day. These cosmic time schemes exist for our benefit, too. Without nighttime sleep we could not function in the day. We need the rhythm of dark and light to experience the harmony of being and the challenge of doing. At night, work ceases and we rest. At daybreak toil resumes—all for the glory of God. Dignifying darkness are the many angelic visits that happen by night (Luke 2:8–14) and the awesome event of Jesus walking then and there on the sea (Matt 14:25).

There are some people who prefer to work the night shift, though by far the majority of us prefer the day. For star-gazers the night sky is an endless source of wonder. This, too, is the time monks and nuns arise to pray. Jesus himself spent long nights in prayer (Matt 14:23; Luke 6:12). Messengers of the mystery were told what to do at night (Ps 16:7); there they meditated (Ps 63:6) and remembered God's name (Ps 119:55). Their mystical actions prove that bright stars need blackness for us to see them. In the words of Saint John of the Cross, the sad night of sensual and spiritual deprivation becomes a glad night, for that is when the union between the lover and the Beloved comes to pass.

Night frees us from the distracting activity of the day. When dusk falls, especially when twilight comes early during the winter, we want nothing more than to light a fire and curl up in front of it. Some nights are sleepless for us. Then we process our troubles and try to reason away our emotional upsets. Weeping in the psalms is a nighttime activity (Ps 6:6; 30:5; 42:3; 77:2). Terror lurks there (Ps

91:5) and in the words of Job, "The night is long, and I am full of tossing until dawn" (Job 7:3–4).

Crimes occur in broad daylight, to be sure, but evil, secrecy, and danger seem to favor the night. The hasty departure of the Chosen People from Egypt occurred in the dark as did the flight of the Holy Family to safety. The arrest and trial of Jesus took place at night and when but after dark would Judas have betrayed him (John 13:30)? That being said, the stillness of the night also fosters creative thoughts and artistic inspirations. Lovemaking happens when the sun goes down. Was it not on a starry night that the infant Jesus came to save us? No wonder the liturgy of midnight mass at Christmas is so popular, when the singing of "Silent Night, Holy Night" may move us to tears and beckon us to pray: *"Lord, when my earthly journey ends, may the boundless light of your glory pierce through death's dark night. Until then, remind me that it is my duty to fulfill the task destined for me in your providential design. Let me operate without hesitation, in unfailing fidelity, to the signals of transcendence I detect in the ordinary. No night is so dark that you are not there with me. Let me place all my trust in you as I await the dawning of a new day and the chance to start over again, knowing that I can only give to others what I have received from you."*

5.

Stars

Dan 12:1–3. . . . But at that time your people shall be delivered, everyone who is found written in the book. Many of those who sleep in the dust of the earth shall awake, some to everlasting life, and some to shame and everlasting contempt. Those who are wise shall shine like the brightness of the sky, and those who lead many to righteousness, like the stars for ever and ever.

Phil 2:14–18. Do all things without murmuring and arguing, so that you may be blameless and innocent, children of God without blemish in the midst of a crooked and perverse generation, in which you shine like stars in the world. It is by your holding fast to the word of life that I can boast on the day of Christ that I did not run in vain or labor in vain. But even if I am being poured out as a libation over the sacrifice and the offering of your faith, I am glad and rejoice with all of you—and in the same way you also must be glad and rejoice with me.

In his masterpiece, *Leaves of Grass*, the poet Walt Whitman describes what it was like for him to be in attendance at a meeting of learned astronomers arguing about the complexity of the cosmos, the distance between the sun and the earth and the accuracy of their equations until he, feeling sick and tired, slipped out of the sweaty room, walked down a darkened lane and from time to time looked up in sheer astonishment at the stars. He treated these heavenly constellations as his personal companions and felt no need at that moment to measure and define them. As God created the sun to rule the day, so stars govern the night. Over eons of time they have enabled explorers to navigate over land and sea, always finding their bearings with the accuracy of a finely calibrated compass.

Stars have a humbling effect upon us. They orient us to the transcendent: "See the highest stars, how lofty they are!" (Job 22:12). Compared to their vastness and perfection, it is no wonder that we feel so insignificant. They evidence the Creator's artistic flare, being more numerous than anyone could count. It is God alone who "determines the number of the stars; he gives to all of them their names" (Ps 147:4). He promises Abraham that his descendants shall be more numerous than the stars, and his promise never goes unfulfilled. References to the stars have an apocalyptic ring. Everlasting life "shall shine . . . like the stars forever and ever" (Dan 12:3). In Revelation 1:20, the seven stars "are the angels of the seven churches" and the twelve stars of the woman in travail identify her as Israel (Rev12:1).

Christ, the morning star (2 Pet 1:19), was born under a twinkling sky that led the Magi to Bethlehem at the time of his birth (Matt 2:2) and drew angelic hosts to sing of the glory of God. If a star marked a new start in earthly history, so too will many stars falling from the sky mark its end (Rev 6:13). In these and similar references in the Bible stars convey and remain full of mystery. They reveal the orderly beauty of God's creation and for experts in the world of physics and astronomy provide an endless source of fascination. They form and reform themselves with galactic power defying our most astute calculations and the telescopes we invent to observe them. They represent the saints in eternal glory, the coronation of Mary as Queen of Heaven, the resplendence of the risen and ascended Lord.

We never fail to refer to famous people as stars and put that symbol on their dressing room doors. Star gazers spend countless hours waiting for the clouds to part so they can point their instruments to the Milky Way and perhaps witness the birth of a new star. Finite as each burning entity is, it seems still to recede to infinity. Who else but our Creator could know them all by name? The special quality of starlight and the stars that form a familiar constellation draw us to look upward. It is as if we are lifted by their light beyond the struggles we face on earth to a place where hope never dies. However burdensome our afflictions may be, we can always aspire to stretch upward to the stars, praying as we do: *"Lord, do not hesitate to take me with you into your living flame of love. In the night I feel your motherly care, your fatherly prayer, multiplied infinitely. Beauty beholding, goodness unfolding. Silence within that whirls out a word. So that is why, O Holy Light, you came to save me one starry night."*

6.

Water

Ezek 36:23–26. I will sanctify my great name, which has been profaned among the nations, and which you have profaned among them; and the nations shall know that I am the Lord, says the Lord God, when through you I display my holiness before their eyes. I will take you from the nations, and gather you from all the countries, and bring you into your own land. I will sprinkle clean water upon you, and you shall be clean from all your uncleannesses, and from all your idols I will cleanse you. A new heart I will give you, and a new spirit I will put within you; and I will remove from your body the heart of stone and give you a heart of flesh.

John 4:13–15. Jesus said to her, 'Everyone who drinks of this water will be thirsty again, but those who drink of the water that I will give them will never be thirsty. The water that I will give will become in them a spring of water gushing up to eternal life.' The woman said to him, 'Sir, give me this water, so that I may never be thirsty or have to keep coming here to draw water.'

Without water everything withers and dies, ourselves included. Drought, such as that experienced in the Holy Land, threatens both agrarian and human life. The Bible reminds us, as in the account of Noah and the flood (Gen 7), that water is subject to God's oversight. This cosmic force can be as life-threatening as it is life-supporting. Symbolic serpents can rise up from the deep to destroy parts of creation but chaos can be replaced by growth and fertility, by the rain that overcomes aridity. Blessings are sealed by water and when God stretches his hand out over the desert it blooms. As the prophet Amos says (5:21–24)," . . . then let justice surge like water and goodness like an unfailing stream."

The early church Father, Tertullian (+222) taught that especially in the sacrament of baptism, water acquires not only the capacity to convey sanctity but also a way to show how central it was to the witness of Jesus. According to Tertullian, as cited in his treatise on ritual washing in the waters of baptism: "Christ was never without water. He himself was baptized with water; when invited to a marriage he inaugurates the exercise of his power with water; when talking he invites the thirsty to partake of his own everlasting water; when teaching about charity he approves among the works of love the offering of a cup of water to a neighbor; he refreshes his strength at the side of a well; he walks on water; he crosses it at will; he uses water to do an act of service to his disciples. This witness to baptism continues right up to the passion. When he is handed over to the cross, water plays a part (witness Pilate's hands); and when he is pierced, water gushes out from his side (witness the soldier's spear)."

The River Jordan and the Sea of Galilee play immense roles in the revelation. Jesus, as Tertullian notes, was baptized in the Jordan and he walked on water to test his disciples' faith. The Samaritan Woman came to draw water from the well and received from Jesus the grace of conversion (John 41:1–42). Even the Dead Sea with its buoyant property is a place of healing, its mud so full of minerals that bathers coat themselves with it. Seasons separate themselves in a land like Israel into rainy and dry. When water is sparse some interpret it as a sign of divine displeasure (I Kgs 8:35); when it is abundant voices sing for joy, praising the Lord who comes to us "like the showers, like the spring rains that water the earth" (Hos 6:3). Lest we make the mistake of equating the supply of rain with the moral state of people, Jesus reminds us that the Father "sends rain on the righteous and on the unrighteous" alike (Matt 5:45).

Waters can be comforting as in a spa but once out of control as in a tsunami they can be perilous. Rogue waves show no mercy, sweeping everything away in their wake. Death by water is a dreadful end. Floods cause unspeakable affliction and everyone begs God for relief. In another vein, the ceremonial effect of cleansing water is immense. It washes away defilement and purifies one's soul. It cleans clothing, food sources, and eating utensils. Impure water, once drunk, can be a source of disease, which is why in a poor country a water purification system is so important. Baptism, a ritual dependent on sprinkling or immersion in holy water, cleanses us of the stain of original sin (Col 2:12). To show his sense of servanthood Jesus washed the feet of his followers. At the start of his pubic life he honored his mother's request to turn water into wine and stretching his hands over a stormy sea he calmed the waves. To believe in him is to find rivers of living water flowing through our own hearts (John 7:38).

This truth reawakens us to the significance of the prophet Isaiah's prediction that "with joy [we] will draw water from the wells of salvation" (12:2–3). To teach us about the power of prayer, Saint Teresa of Avila uses the analogy of the "four waters," leading us from vocal to mental to quiet to contemplative prayer. From hauling water up from the well with a bucket, to using a windlass to lessen our labor, to devising a system of irrigation to water our garden, to waiting without any effort on our part for the rain to fall, she teaches us how to pray in union with the life-giving stream of God's word. For Teresa, his Majesty is the cosmic gardener watering his creation (Ps 104:13–16), the healer washing us clean and making us whiter than snow. We do our part when we ladle cold water from a well and offer it to one who thirsts (Matt 10:42). God repeats the benefits of the waters of purification when we accept the grace of forgiveness and shed tears of repentance, saying, *"Lord, let the oneness I feel in your presence cascade through my being as rain drops from high places, wetting desert spaces and teaching me the efficacy of tears of sorrow and joy poured out of my interiority and poured into the healing 'presence of the Lord'"* (Lam 2:19).

7.

Wind

I Kgs 19:11–13. He said, 'Go out and stand on the mountain before the Lord, for the Lord is about to pass by.' Now there was a great wind, so strong that it was splitting mountains and breaking rocks in pieces before the Lord, but the Lord was not in the wind; and after the wind an earthquake, but the Lord was not in the earthquake; and after the earthquake a fire, but the Lord was not in the fire; and after the fire a sound of sheer silence. When Elijah heard it, he wrapped his face in his mantle and went out and stood at the entrance of the cave. Then there came a voice to him that said, 'What are you doing here, Elijah?'

Acts 2:1–4. When the day of Pentecost had come, they were all together in one place. And suddenly from heaven there came a sound like the rush of a violent wind, and it filled the entire house where they were sitting. Divided tongues, as of fire, appeared among them, and a tongue rested on each of them. All of them were filled with the Holy Spirit and began to speak in other languages, as the Spirit gave them ability.

Like the wind rushing by at various speeds—from gentle breezes to hurricane force fury—so the Spirit of God blows how and where it will. Wind, though unseen, is felt in our faces and at our back. It can cool the hottest day or heat an already sweltering desert with its own brand of devastating dust storms. So powerful can the wind be that we try to harvest it in modern-day turbines to generate electrical currents. Windmills still help their operators to redirect the water supply or to grind grain. We listen to the haunting sound of wind blowing through the trees, rattling a loose shutter or tearing off a topcoat or hat or turning an umbrella inside out. Wind shows no mercy for what it carries away in a tornado. In one fell swoop it can devastate the terrain on which it touches down.

When we want to describe an activity as useless, we say that he or she is chasing after the wind since one's efforts produce no effects at all. How useless it is to try to capture the wind between our fingers. The result is wholly unsubstantial like filling one's belly with the hot east wind (Job 15:2). Only when God speaks out of the whirlwind does Job cease to question his destiny. In a similar vein, the prophet Isaiah predicts that our sins will sweep us away like the wind (64:6). Then, too, Jesus says that when we build our house on sand instead of on solid rock the winds will blow against it and beat it into the dust (Matt 7:24–27). So it is for the person who does not hear the word of God and keep it. That is why the Apostle Paul warns us that we must grow from the infancy to the maturity of the Christian life less we risk being "blown here and there by every wind of teaching" (Eph 4:14).

The wind with which we associate the Holy Spirit is like a warm breath, blowing out aspirations and inhaling inspirations. When we want to encourage people to get on with their lives, we advise them to put a little more wind into their sails. God, the master of the winds, keeps them in his "storehouse" and only when he so commands do they emerge and blow where he sends them (Ps 104:4; 148:8). Judgment is foretold in the prophet Jeremiah as a time when "a scorching wind from the barren heights in the desert" is sent from God (4:11–12). Wind can be either punishing or beneficial, catastrophic or cooling. God will scatter his foes to the four winds (North, South, East, and West), but he will also gather the lost under his wings and over the valley of dry bones breathe the breath of life: " . . . breathe into these slain, that they may live" (Ezek 37:9).

It is the Spirit who breathes new life into body and soul and leads us to unfold the hidden plan of God. When fears of such radical obedience overtake us, we have to toss them to the wind. The day Jesus died on Mount Calvary, the wind blew with such ferocity that all but his mother and a few stalwart disciples scattered. To follow him we have to bypass the anxiety we feel and recommit ourselves to go forward into the wind of his saving word, praying with every breath we breathe, *"Lord, let me head into the wind that sweeps the desert clean of falsehood and deceit. Convince me of the truth that compunction blows away the dust of sin. Then the wind of your forgiveness scatters like thistles the last fragments of forgetfulness. Guide me to the wholeness that dispels useless ego-defenses and implants the seeds of perfect trust in my soul."*

Epilogue

But ask the animals, and they will teach you;
The birds of the air, and they will tell you;
And the fish of the sea will declare to you.
Who among all these does not know that the hand of the
Lord has done this?
In his hand is the life of every living thing
And the breath of every human being (Job 12:7–10).

In her masterpiece of the mystical life, *The Interior Castle*, Teresa of Avila identifies one of God's creatures that symbolizes for her the entire process of transformation. It is the silkworm that offers her a vivid and accurate description of the journey of the soul from the cocoon stage through that of metamorphosis to the emergence of the butterfly.

The silkworm in the first stages of transformation draws energy from the heat which comes from the Holy Spirit. Personal prayer and the reception of Holy Communion protect the soul like the cocoon builds a shield around the life within to make sure transformation will occur and the butterfly will emerge.

Like the silkworm, the soul dwells in a place where she dies a death that marks the onset of her rebirth. The cocoon for Teresa is likened to Christ under whose embrace a worm, once wrinkled and ugly, turns into a beautiful butterfly. Now, thanks to the action of its Beloved, the soul can fly away from the safety of the cocoon and not be lost. The soul has been set free and transformed by love. She cannot return to her previous state but neither can she deny that some force greater than she urges her to go forward to that place of grace where she lives no longer as an independent "I" but as a Christ-formed soul since the Beloved himself now lives in her.

So fully did Teresa enter into this contemplation of creation that deep truths of nature and grace were revealed to her by God. She saw through a kaleidoscope of revelations rooted in creation how God works in our souls and in all living things. As recipients of his favors, we catch a glimpse of what awaits us in heaven "without the intervals, trials, and dangers that there are in this tempestuous sea."

With Saint Teresa, we, too, turn our attention to our Creator each time we see and celebrate another manifestation of the love that embraces us everywhere in creation. Echoing her sentiments we pray, *"Lord, may it please you to see how much I want what I do to be of service to you. My faults and failings are no match for your grace. On the blackboard of life, in its first revelation in creation, teach me to read every message inscribed by your loving hand. Then the good you ask of me will be the legacy I leave to those entrusted to my care. May each of us come to see in every epiphany of your mystery the deep truth taught by Saint Teresa that God alone suffices."*